AF326551

My War, My Art

My War, My Art

Ovidio Garcia

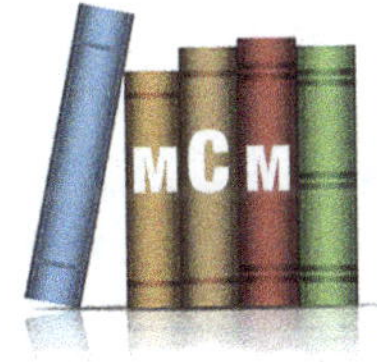

MCM Books

February 2019

Patricia Ann Saldaña typed the manuscript and Al Gómez photographed the artwork.

Published in the United States by MCM Books, Hutto, Texas.
All rights reserved.

ISBN: 978-0-9967473-3-2

Library of Congress Control Number: 2018959584

DEDICATION

To my wife Elma C. Garcia, without whose support I could not have done this.

and

To Veterans of all wars.

Foreword

Ovidio Garcia tells us in his introduction that, during his two tours as an airborne infantryman in Vietnam (1966–67, 1970–71), he saw only one army photographer "and he was killed on his second day of insertion into his unit" and that personal cameras were not allowed because of "intelligence factors." He learned only many years later that there were soldiers whose military occupational specialty was "artist." He himself never saw one.

Garcia suffers from post-traumatic stress disorder. Over many years now, he has tried to paint or draw reassuringly simple and honest scenes and impressions of his memories. These images in mixed media, ink, and water colors are presented in *My War, My Art*, accompanied each by a few paragraphs with titles like "Recollection of a Premonition," "Three Stooges Skit," "Alas, Poor Yorick," "Dak To," "Tree of Life," and "War Dogs." Captions in red font gloss his artwork. We are told that, for instance, though the "Tree of Life" was "Not the Disney World Tree," it did give him and his fellow soldiers some protection from big, black elephant leeches that overnight attached themselves to the roof of his mouth causing him to awake choking on his own blood. The leeches attacked a fellow infantryman in the worst possible place for men in battle (or not)—his penis.

Garcia and his buddies climbed the tree to escape the booby traps and guerrillas of the natural world itself.

When we pick up a new book about war, many questions come to mind: was the author a soldier, a doctor or a nurse, a war correspondent or photographer, a combat artist, or a civilian survivor who witnessed other civilians becoming statistical members of that morally grotesque and euphemistic category known as "collateral damage." Why did any of them write? What (if anything) are they trying to tell us? Or are they writing only for an inner circle of brothers (and now sisters) in arms, who know all too well the realities of war and hold its truths sacred?

Robert Graves stated flatly that his poems about World War I were meant for men "bound to one another by [the] suicidal sacrament" of trench warfare. For others, he wrote prettified tales full of untruths they could read and believe. Journalist and screenwriter William Broyles, a Vietnam veteran, has written that the point of a soldier's or veteran's war stories "is not to enlighten but to exclude [those who have not been to war]; its message is not its content, but putting the listener in his place."

Do authors who suffered or witnessed the violence of war write primarily for themselves, to capture what they once saw and still see in their minds? Or "just to get the sight out of their heads." In World War I, an Australian officer who witnessed his men being slaughtered like cattle in a stockyard during the battle of the Somme called it "murder" plain and simple, in "a place so terrible a raving lunatic could never imagine the horror …."

It often takes a long time for survivors of war to decide to tell their stories and to figure out how exactly to do so in words, melodies, or pictures. Joseph Heller's *Catch-22* (1961) appeared sixteen years after World War II; Kurt Vonnegut Jr.'s *Slaughterhouse-Five* (1969) twenty-four years afterward. Rolando Hinojosa-Smith in his Korean *Love Songs* conveyed plainly and simply the surreally cold-blooded savagery of his war twenty-five years after the fact: "there it is," his poems say.

Khe Sanh veteran Charles Patterson needed fifteen years to complete a poem he began after a friend in his unit was killed in combat. Only then had the residue of war and the passage of time produced a kind of understanding and the deep human feeling he had to put into words. For some "war writers" that feeling reflects a need for closure. For others, it involves an opening up at long last to themselves or others.

The US National Archives makes available online thousands of photographs, paintings, drawings, and films depicting wars in which Americans have fought and died from the Civil War to what we call the Iraq War. Eyewitnesses have, of course, always produced written accounts, published or not, of warfare. For example, the (University of Texas) Harry Ransom Center houses some of Tom Lea's World War II collected images and notebooks. But rarely are visual images and written narratives produced by the same hands.

We have now received from the heart and soul of Ovidio Garcia a gift he has wrapped for us a half century after he fought in Vietnam. He was inspired by the simple watercolor images that Samuel Chamberlain drew from memories and imaginings of his time as a mounted rifleman with the forces of Gen. Zachary Taylor in 1846–47. Unlike the highly romanticized stories Chamberlain wrote (separately from his paintings), Garcia's forthright accounts of his time in Vietnam convey the same anguish and matter-of-fact resignation that Charles Patterson felt in the years just before his recent death. Explaining to students in one of my classes why he wrote his poems, Patterson described motives like those of Garcia:

> I just wrote my image of my memories and hoped that they would help someone else understand a little of how war "felt." For the first time I think that I have begun to understand what I have written about. Every war is a tragedy for everyone. There are no winners or losers; there is no good, no evil. There is just sudden death or injury on both sides. One moment a man is alive the next he's a corpse regardless of whose army he is fighting in or even if he is fighting, or if a civilian steps on a forgotten mine ten years later. We fought for no better reason than we were there and had to do it.

Garcia's stories and images of his experience in Vietnam are prose equivalents of Hinojosa-Smith's unvarnished poetry about Korea. Both men just want to tell us how it was. As Garcia sums it up: "Dere it is".

Garcia's pictures and words vividly evoke the true premonition of death that kept him from boarding a Chinook helicopter that crashed shortly afterward; a mother's constant love for her two sons fighting an unfathomable war on the far side of the planet, even though they rarely wrote to her; relentless leeches in streams and trees; seriocomic encounters with the enemy that could have brought death; friendly fire transforming wounded soldiers into corpses; a foot, complete with sandal, detached from a Viet Cong guerrilla who escaped into the jungle; and the pitiful tale of the hapless North Vietnamese nineteen-year-old who knew less about surviving in a jungle than even the rawest American teenage recruit in Garcia's unit.

All these images were seared into Garcia's psyche by post-traumatic stress. *My War, My Art* is, therefore, a tribute to his endurance and devotion to the men he served beside and to the veterans and non-veterans who have not and will not look away from the truths he has courageously put on display in this book.

Ovidio Garcia, like many who steadfastly put others ahead of themselves, is too modest about what he has created here. His drawing "Bad Dreams" and related story "B52 Bomb Blast" (20–21) called to my mind Francisco Goya's etching *Esto es peor* (this is worse), an emblem of the repulsive trials of war that have haunted our collective memories for two hundred years.

Thomas G. Palaima
University of Texas–Austin

Introduction

Doctors at the VA diagnosed me as having post-traumatic stress disorder commonly referred to as PTSD. Now I understand why I do some of the things I do; I am trying to cope with memories that are embedded in my subconscious forever. Such as, "I should have done this," or "if I had done that." This understanding comes with a generous amount of survivor's guilt. It got so bad at one point that if it were not for intensive counseling and the support of my spouse I'm not sure I would be here today. Even as I write now, I tear up, and my anxiety level goes through the roof.

After reading Samuel Chamberlain's *My Confession: Recollections of a Rogue* and greatly enjoying his paintings and sketches of the Mexican American War, I was inspired to do the same. He has never been acclaimed as a great artist, but his paintings now hang in various art museums across the nation, almost a century and a half later. Like my drawings, they were the primitive artistic depictions of an enlisted soldier who was there and then put his recollections on canvas.

In my two tours in Vietnam, I saw only one Army photographer, and he was killed on the second day of his insertion into his unit. Personal cameras were not allowed in front-line infantry units because of the apparent intelligence factor. Some still carried cameras. On several occasions we found dead enemy soldiers with cameras in their possession which we believed they had taken from our brothers killed in action. The only personal photos that I have were taken by a visitor to the forward area. Many years later I found out that there were soldiers whose MOS (military occupational specialty) was as artists, but I never saw one.

Like Chamberlain, I hope to tell the story of my personal experiences during a traumatic period of my life. These events are hard-wired into my brain and I still struggle with many unanswered questions. Why am I still alive when better men are dead? Why didn't I get on the helicopter that fell out of the sky killing everyone on board, one of the worst Army aviation crashes? Was it ESP? I distinctly remember the premonition; I didn't like the aircraft, didn't like the way it lumbered, the way it maneuvered to land, slow and cumbersome. I considered the repercussions and disobeyed the order to board it. Thirty men died and I'm still alive. Why?

On another occasion, due to my impulsive nature, I intentionally jumped between two enemy soldiers. I relive this event everyday. How could they have possibly missed me? The ends of our rifle barrels were hitting each other. They're long dead, and I'm alive. Why? Someday I'll know the reason why. When my time comes and I meet my creator, who has given me the ability to bring this endeavor to fruition, I will thank Him for letting me live this long, and for letting me see my kids and grandkids grow up.

Many veterans of the Vietnam War have told me they never saw the enemy up close or did not see them at all. As an airborne infantryman, a paratrooper, that did two tours in that unfortunate place, one with the 101st Brigade from 1966-1967 and the other with the 173rd Airborne Brigade from 1970-1971, my experiences were indeed different.

I offer those experiences to the reader in artistic depictions and written accounts of what transpired at that moment in time, as I remember them. I drew most of the sketches after I left the Army and I managed to hang on to them through the thick and thin of my life. One of the reasons it took me so long to write this book is because I make no pretense of being a historical writer with dates, places, and the strategies of operations. Those details never concerned me.

I drew these artistic accounts because they remind me of experiences which weigh heavy on me in a very unique way. I thought that they would never see the light of day, but after much encouragement from other veterans and non-veterans, and favorable results at many public showings, here they are, or resorting to a favorite phrase used in Vietnam to end a conversation "Dere it is!"

Table of Contents

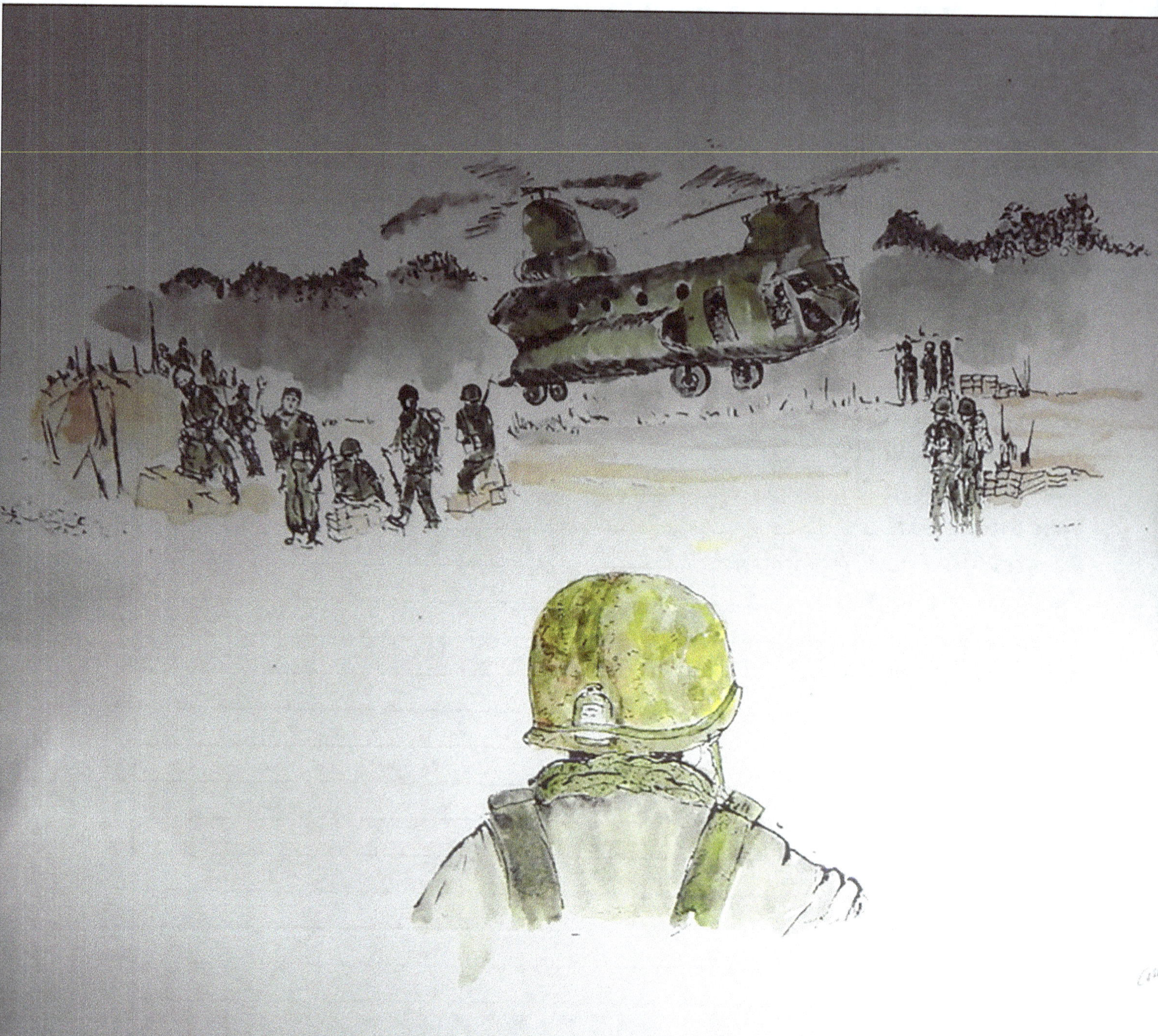

Recollection of a Premonition

As I waited for the incoming Chinook helicopter to transport me along with three other troopers, mostly replacements being ferried out to a jungle forward area, I was looking at the 101st brigade forward landing zone, the LZ as we called it.

Specialist 4th Class Swayze, a kid I knew from my unit, was bitching that he only had two weeks to do in-country before his tour would be up. The new first sergeant had cleared the rear area of all the sick, lame, and lazy, including me. I had just arrived back from the hospital after being treated for a wound, so I empathized with Swayze.

Then I noticed a group of tents about a 100 yards away, on the opposite side of our unit and asked Swayze what unit was there? He told me, and I remembered that my homey Sgt. Carlos Torres was in that unit. I told Swayze I'd be back and went to see if Sgt. Torres was around. The first guy I asked told me that Sgt. Torres had stepped on a land mine the day before and was on his way out of Vietnam.

I had started back to the LZ when I heard the Chinook. I had never flown in one. I looked at it long and hard. I didn't like the sound and how cumbersome it seemed as it aligned itself over the LZ. I got this feeling of apprehension, like when I walked point. I had a premonition of death if I got on this helicopter.

I stopped a distance away and watched the ramp come down and everyone load up, Swayze being the last one. He motioned for me to come. I didn't. Death spared me. When I finally get to meet Death face-to-face I will thank it for that. All my life, I have wondered "why?"

A premonition of death.

My Cahn

I arrived in the Republic of South Vietnam on 1 February 1966 with orders assigning me to the 173rd Airborne, the best unit in the U.S. Army as far as I was concerned. There I was supposed to join old friends who had trained and partied with me on Okinawa. I had missed their deployment from there to Vietnam months before.

From Okinawa, I could have returned to the States but I volunteered to go directly to the theatre of war. Why? Because of my father's saying "Anda para que no te platiquen." ("Go so you won't hear it from someone else.")

At the 90th replacement company in Saigon, which by the way I was never close to again, I was shanghaied to the 101st. I'll never forget that conversation. A staff sergeant came up to me and said, "You got a choice. You can go the 1st Cavalry or the 101st."

I said, "No, I'm going to the 173rd. I've got the orders in my pocket."

Cool and calm he answered, "You didn't hear me Buck Sergeant. You're going to the 1st Cavalry or the 101st."

Six days later after going from Base Camp Phang Rang to the forward area at Tuy Hoa and then, hurriedly, with a very dirty M16 which I didn't get to zero for accuracy, I joined my unit Charlie Company, Second 502 Airborne Infantry Battalion, 1st Brigade, 101st Airborne Division. I arrived as they were assaulting a village called My Canh and, as I would realize later, I was missing an essential item; jungle boots because they didn't have my size.

I was young and anxious to get there. I was an unassigned replacement moving with the company commander's entourage composed of artillery forward fire observers, engineer liaisons, and about four radio operators. I saw the fire coming out of the village tree line and then we answered with Napalm, artillery, and helicopter gunships.

I kept my wits about me, because shortly after we arrived I overheard radio chatter saying that a Sgt. Garcia and others were KIA as they had approached the village that triggered the

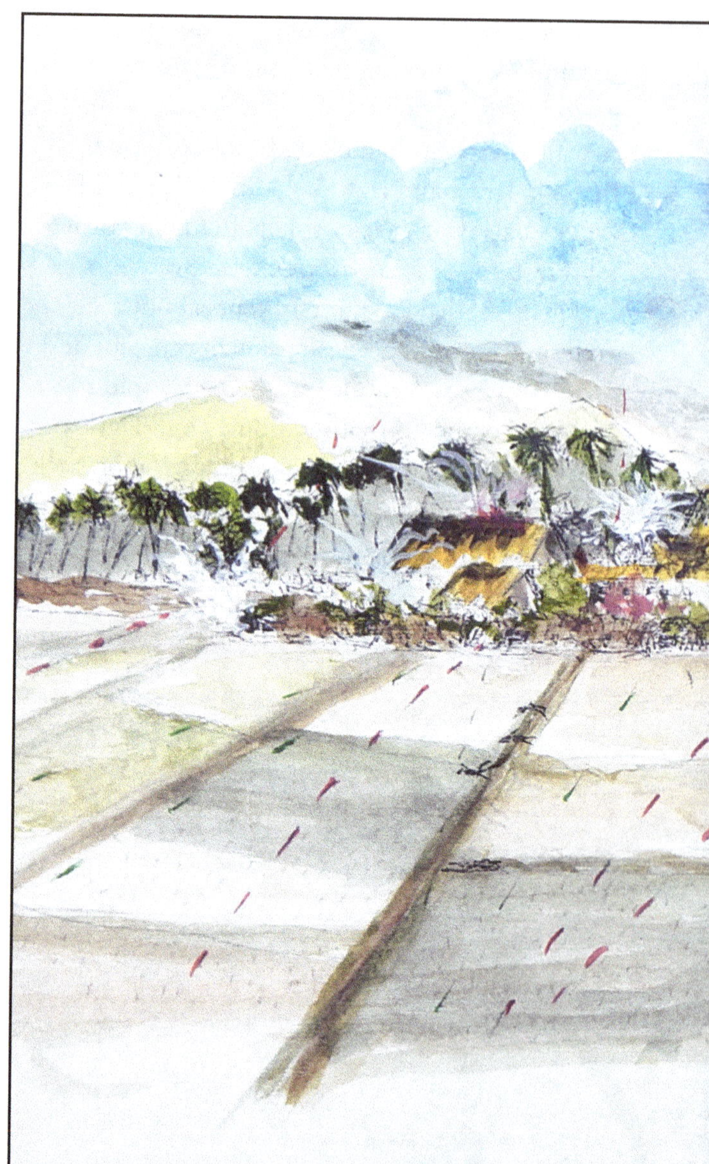

action. Later I learned that Sgt. Garcia's full name was David Garcia from Colorado, an E-5 Buck Sergeant, like me.

As bad as it might sound, that news gave me the fortitude to persevere through that two-day battle because I thought that the odds of two Garcías getting killed in the same action were in my favor. I did not see any enemy close enough to fire at so I never fired my weapon. Instead, I carried ammunition and helped with the wounded.

Later, as we went through the village, we saw plenty of dead, mostly civilians. This was before the phrase "collateral damage" was coined. I felt sorry for them.

That action at My Canh earned a the platoon leader who led the assault that breached the defensive perimeter a posthumous Congressional Medal of Honor. He was the first recipient of the Medal of Honor for the 101st in Vietnam.

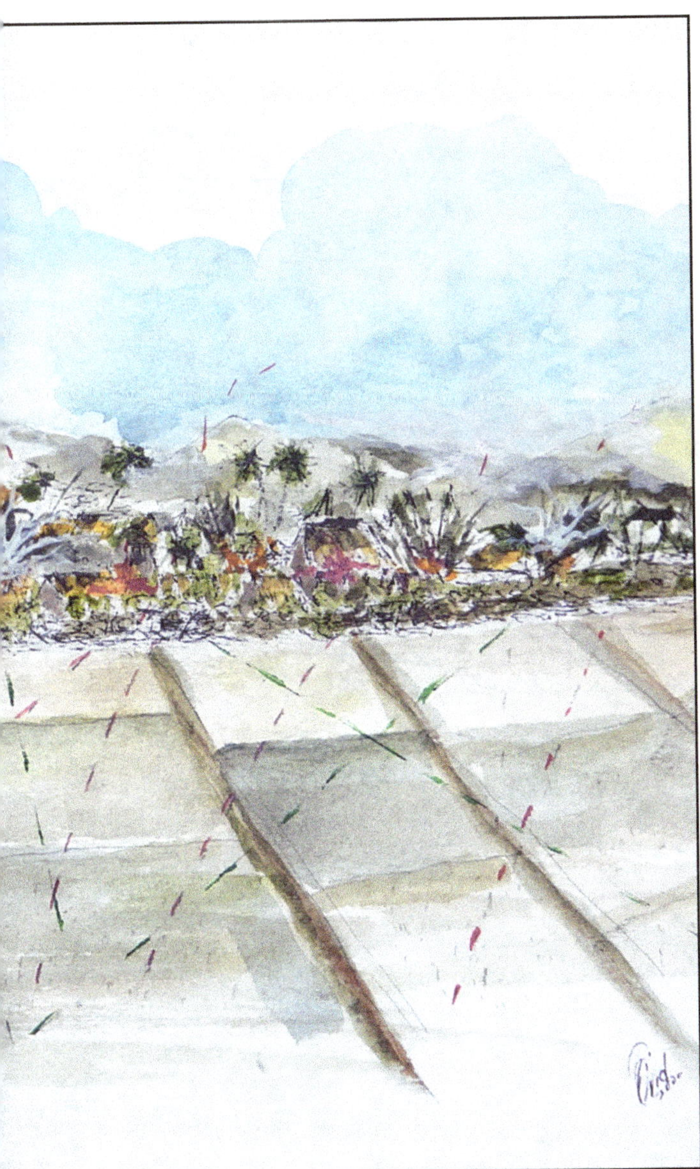

My introduction to the war.

For many years after my Vietnam war experiences, I could not see a tree-line without searching for possible enemy positions. The natural features set off a mental response that involuntarily sent me back to particular incidents that caused loss of lives and limbs. It was an involuntary reaction. My imagination would run wild. How could I approach it without exposing myself?

For a long time tree-lines caused me to relive running towards a village in the tree-line. If I had

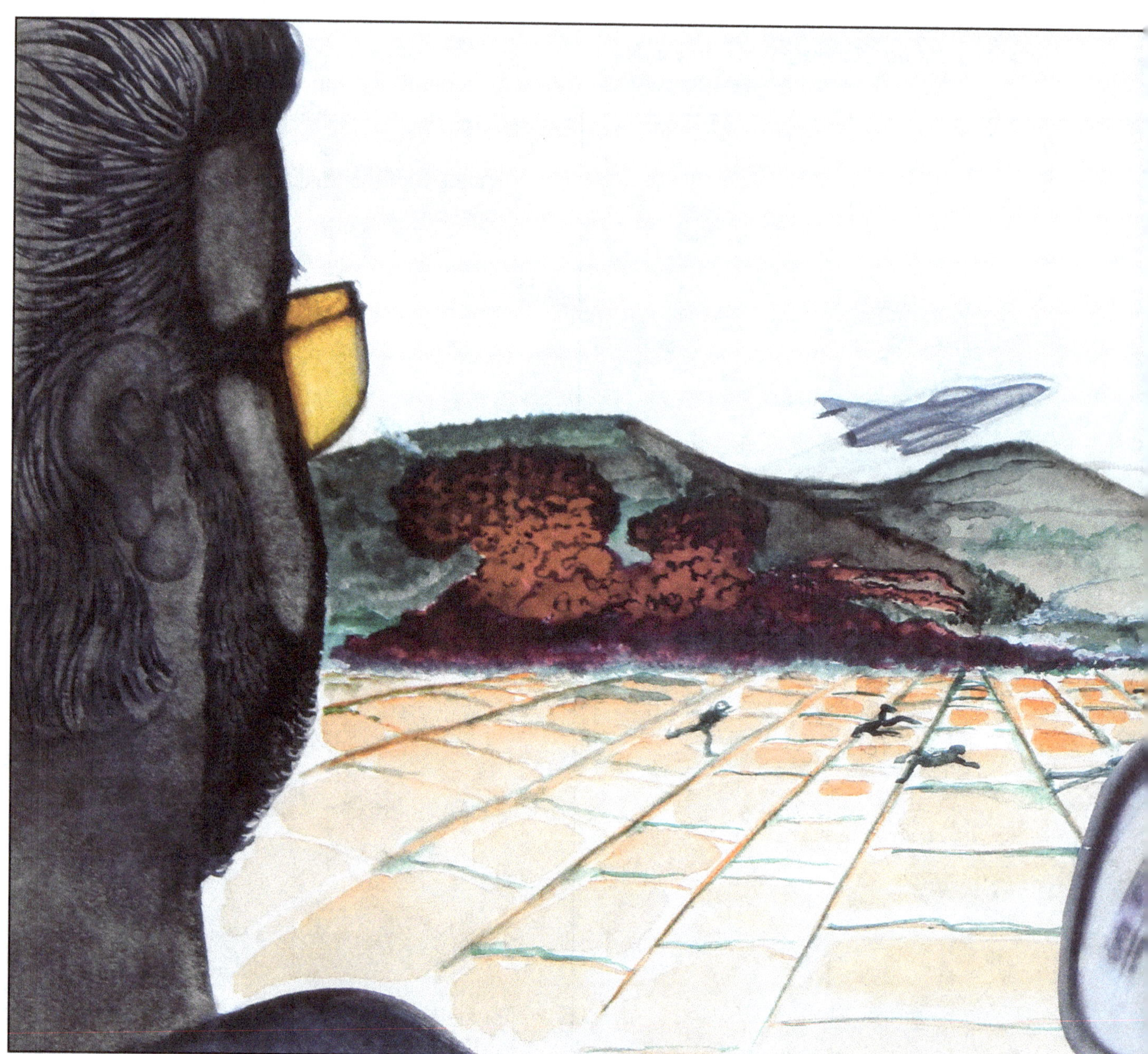

FFERENT TO ME

done this or that, perhaps some of my men would still be alive. I became oblivious of everything except the scene being replayed in my mind. Looking for possible cover and concealed ways to approach it, sometimes I could imagine the aerial

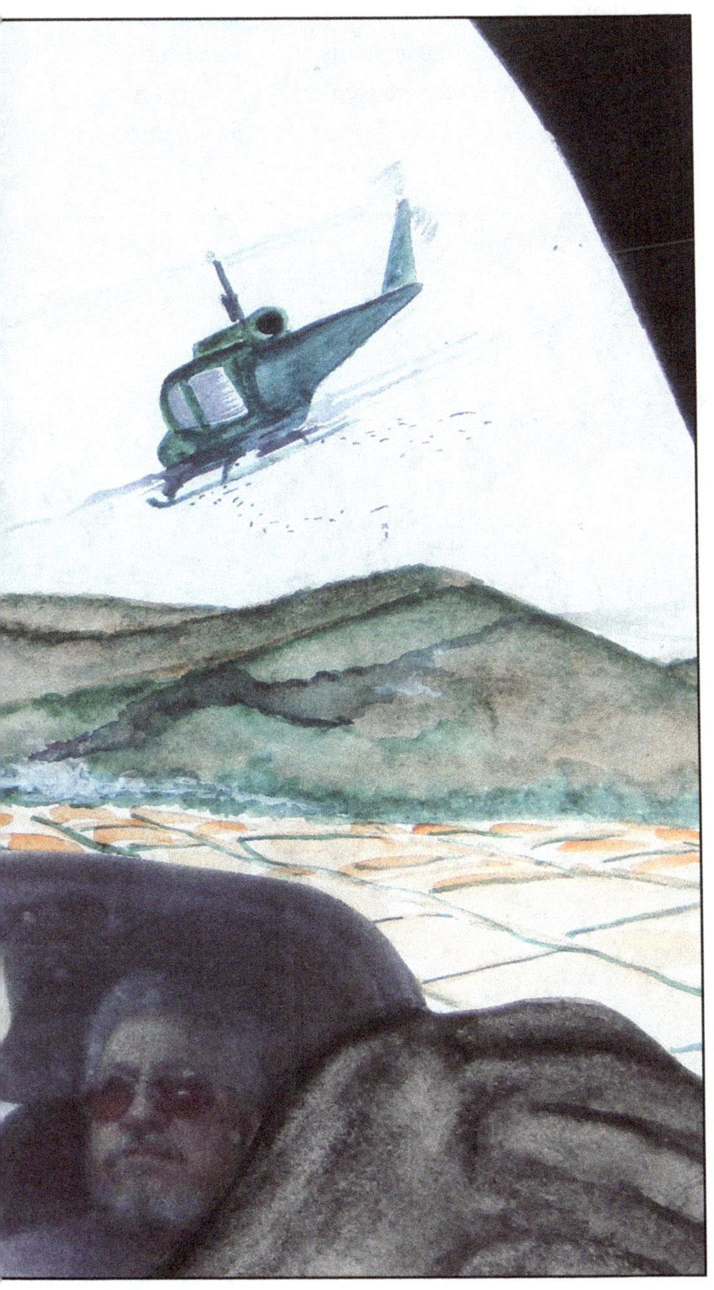

and artillery support pounding the tree-line. I still see the vapor around the jet's engines as it climbed after dropping napalm. I hear the distinct roar of the Huey gunships firing into the enemy positions. I am caught in a time warp.

Talk about a driving distraction. Driving for me was a hazard as I could not prevent these intrusive thoughts of "what if?" I knew that there was something wrong with me I just did not know what it was.

As an infantry squad leader when I led a patrol I was responsible; so approaching a tree-line, I was upfront with my point man. Crossing a stream or river, I thought this is when they would open fire catching us in the middle of the river or the clearing.

In those moments, with every step I took, I knew it might be my last one. But I did it anyway without my men knowing my inner fears and having them lose their trust in me. For every patrol leader, there was no more significant responsibility than his men. All my training prepared me towards that, and it took effect.

Some military experts will tell you that soldiers are trained to follow the orders of their appointed leaders. But in real time it does not always work like that. Men willingly follow leaders they trust. My men knew that I would never order them to do something I would not do.

Even today as I drive around South Texas and come across a clearing with a tree line at the far end, my mind races to Vietnam and another time when this scene was framed with danger.

Sometime in February 1967, during a search and destroy operation clearing a populated valley, I was the point for a rifle company element. Going alongside the valley floor in one direction we heard gunfire ahead.

Later, we met another platoon coming from the opposite direction on the other side of the narrow valley. The platoon leader informed us they had received sniper fire from our side of the valley up ahead and it had held them up, but they had taken no casualties. We continued, and about 200 yards ahead, I spied what I thought was a farmer walking alongside a shrub fence line towards some houses on the opposite side. He was walking nonchalantly with his farm tool on his shoulder; probably just going home to mamasan after a hard day's labor. As I watched him, I remembered my days working in farm fields and almost felt a kinship with him until he twirled the tool on his shoulder and instead of a hoe or pick, it was a rifle.

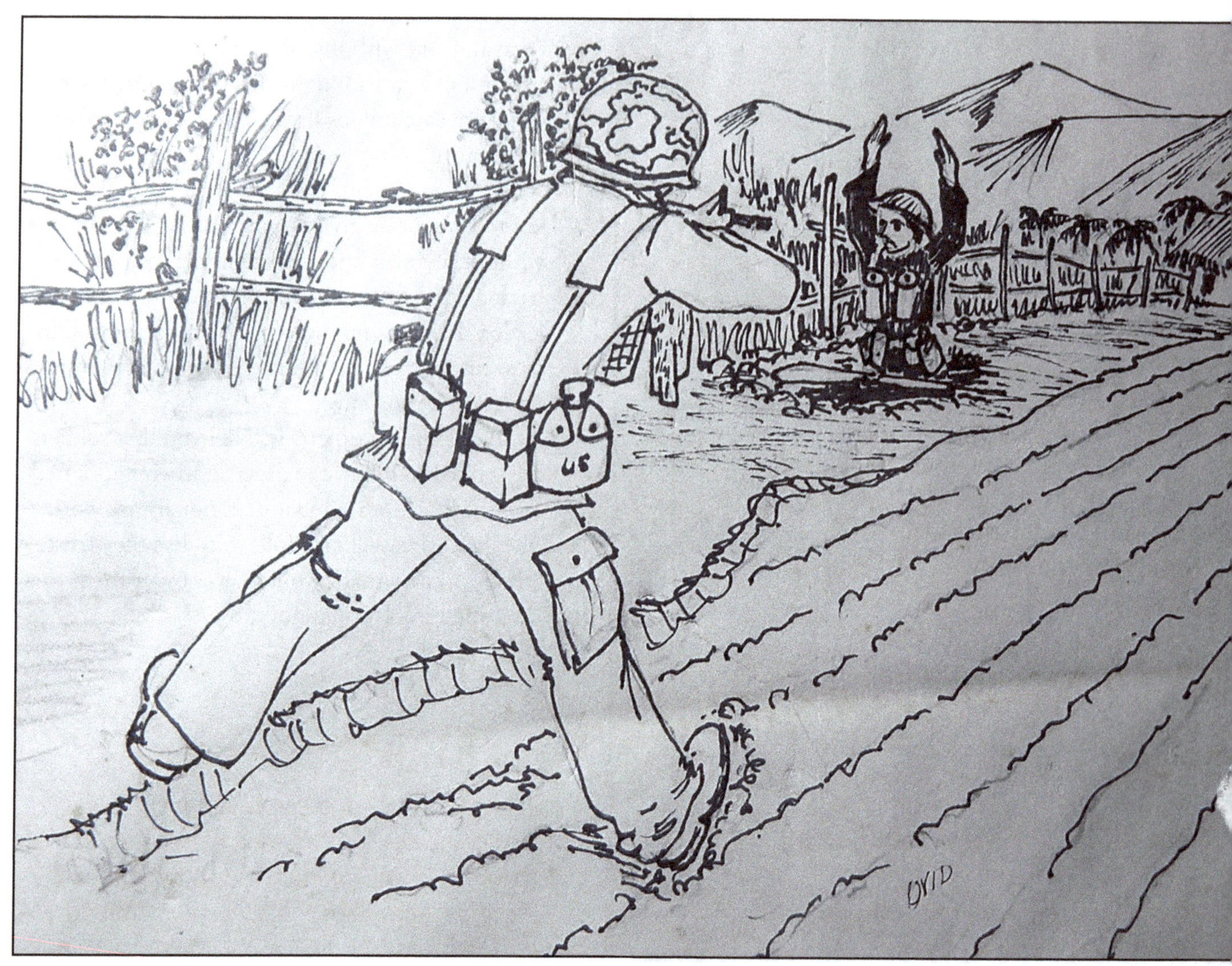

WEEK OFF

All kinship and fellow worker thoughts left my mind and hatred of snipers took over. I fired a long burst at him. He disappeared behind the hedge fence, but I was sure I had hit him. I went around the end of the fence, but there he was standing in a hole alongside the path, about 50 feet away, pointing a Mauser rifle at me.

I squeezed the trigger on my weapon, trying to beat his shot, but my weapon was empty. Earlier, I had fired another burst and was going to pay the price now. Still aiming at me, I noticed he was an older fellow, well outfitted, dressed in solid black. As I took all this in, there was no time for fear. He was taking too long to shoot.

I started shouting "Dung lo, dung lo," hoping he would surrender as I asked. While pointing my empty weapon at him, he deliberately, slowly set his weapon on the ground and put his arms up. I made a record time magazine change and I had the power of life or death over him, but I decided to let him live, despite his sniper status, because he hadn't hit anyone from our unit, and because of his comportment.

Shortly after, no more than 100 yards away, while going by a cornfield I heard rustling and saw stalks moving. I signaled the guys behind to stop. I went in and found another one in uniform, but no weapon. Now I had two prisoners.

The battalion commander Col. Emerson landed shortly after. He was beside himself with two POWs. The medic who had been helping me keep my boots together with surgical tape rubber wanted me to take my boots off and show the Colonel my feet. I did. The soles of my feet had turned black.

The Colonel jumped back and wanted to know whose fault it was. I told him they didn't have jungle boots my size when I came through the rear. My platoon Sargent hemmed and hawed trying to make an excuse for not ordering some for me. Truth is we didn't like each other. I was the first replacement among a group of guys that had come together as a unit from the States. They didn't like my recklessness, as they called it. That rift remained until they started getting more replacements.

The result was my parade field paratrooper's boots didn't last a month in the jungle. I caught a disease that affected my feet off and on for forty years. This jungle rot got me a week's downtime in the rear and a new pair of boots.

A very sharp looking sniper.

A Mother's Prayer

My brother, Hector Garcia was badly wounded on Vietnam and was awared the Purple Heart medal. After long medical treatment and therapy, he returned to civilian life. He joined the U.S. Post Office in 1973, and his first assignment was to the Port-Ayers Mail Station, in Corpus Christi, Texas, which delivered to our neighborhood. Adan Chavez, our neighborhood mailman, helped train him as a carrier.

Adan once told Hector how much he hated to go by our house without mail from us.

"Neither you nor your brother wrote very much," Adan told Hector in a sad tone. He recalled how my mother waited faithfully on the porch every day for his arrival. He never forgot her look of disappointment or elation when he made his "mail call."

In Hector's eyes, our mother will always be the true veteran in our family. She prayed for our father who served in World War II. She prayed for me during two tours in Vietnam. Then, she prayed for Hector.

On one occasion, while home on leave before being shipped to Vietnam, Hector had a nightmare. All he remembers was waking up in our mother's arms.

"I was soaking wet with sweat," Hector recalls. "I remember dad and mother asking what the dream was about. They said I had been cussing loud. For some reason, I couldn't remember the dream."

Shortly after arriving in Vietnam, Hector's unit walked into an ambush while on patrol.

"The first round flew by, inches from my face," he remembers. "I could feel the heat and power of the bullet. Then the shit hit the fan. I began to run for cover, and as I ran, I was hit twice on my leg. It was then that the dream became clear to me. It was the nightmare I had before. I knew I wasn't going to die; I was safe in my mother's arms."

I want to thank my mother Carmen López García snd other veterans mothers for loving us and praying for us.

Our mother will always be the true veteran in our family.

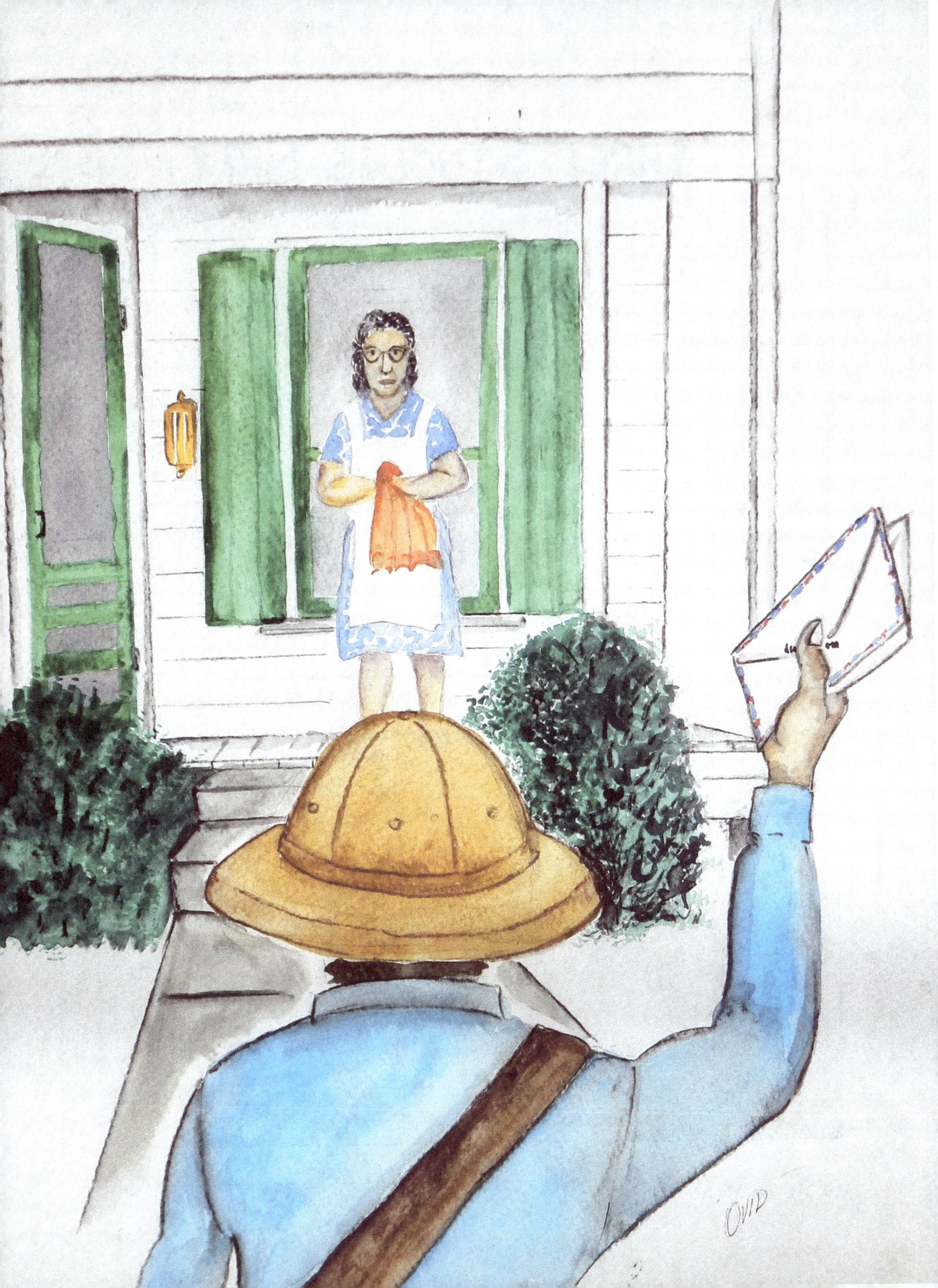

THREE STOOGES SKIT

In April 1966, after walking the hills for two weeks with no enemy contact, we were coming down from the high ground looking for a clearing that could serve as an extraction point. We were the company lead squad, and I was the point back-up for a new, overweight replacement. We stopped on the trail to take five and readjust our gear.

I saw Brown, the point man, go down on one knee and aim his weapon at a point around a turn in the trail we were following. I ran to the turn as I saw Brown fumbling with his rifle and there were two NVA soldiers with large, five-gallon cans on top of their heads looking at us. I brought my weapon up to fire at the one directly in front of me.

I had cleared and locked my weapon at the onset of the break, believing we were secure enough to do this. I pulled the trigger, and nothing happened. I rammed the charging handle and, at this point, the Viet was still looking at me. I pulled the trigger again, and again nothing! The safety was still on.

The enemy then threw his can at me but he missed me, but its contents of rice did not. I blinked. When I opened my eyes, the Viets were fleeing around the next corner. I fired, but they were gone. All during this time, Brown was still fumbling with his jammed weapon.

I couldn't help but think that the scene was straight out of a Three Stooges movie.

Rice husks in my eyes.

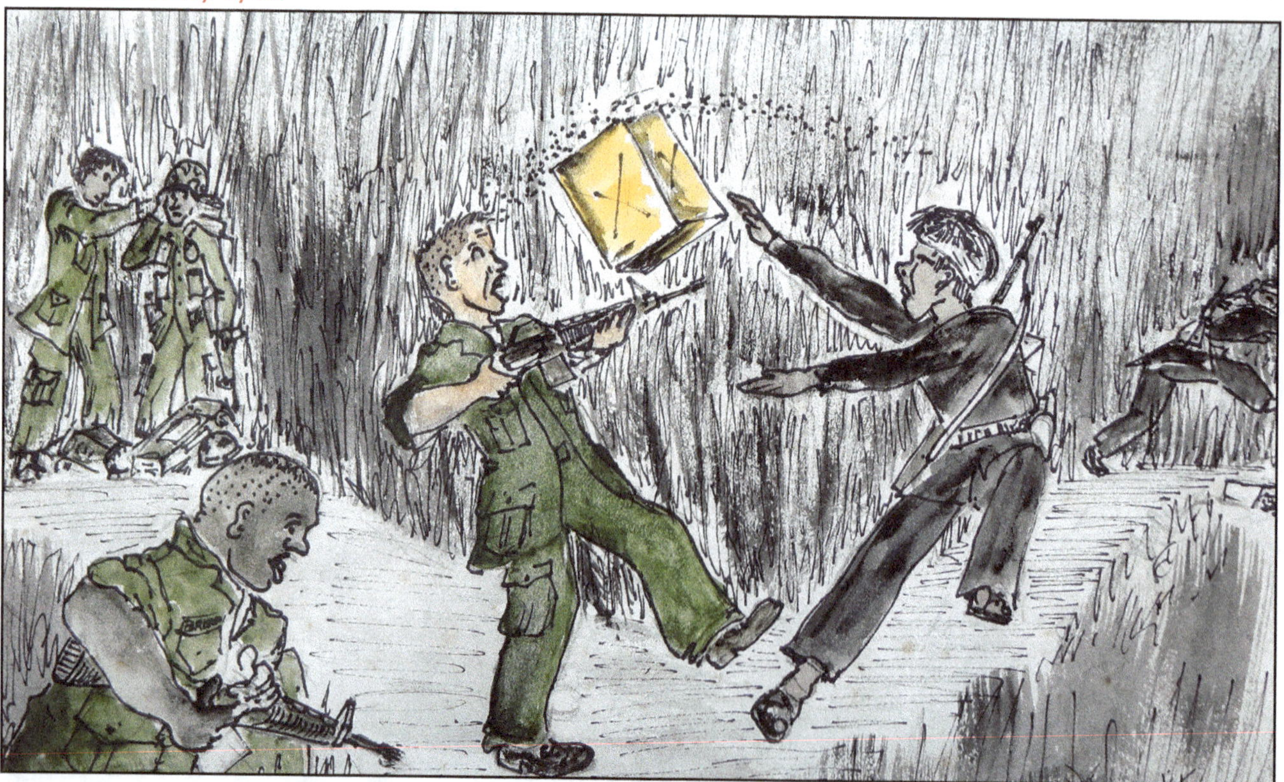

Raindrops Keep Falling on My Head

I n March 1971 we operated in an area that was unlike any other that we had ever seen. It looked surreal. Everything was blackened.

There was no life form. We could not even see bugs. We ate in it. We slept in it. We breathed it in. Our bodies were covered by "soot" which was hard to remove.

We were not acquainted with defoliants. It was much later before we learned that it was Agent Orange.

The four horsemen of Vietnam: diabetes, cancer, heart problems and PTSD.

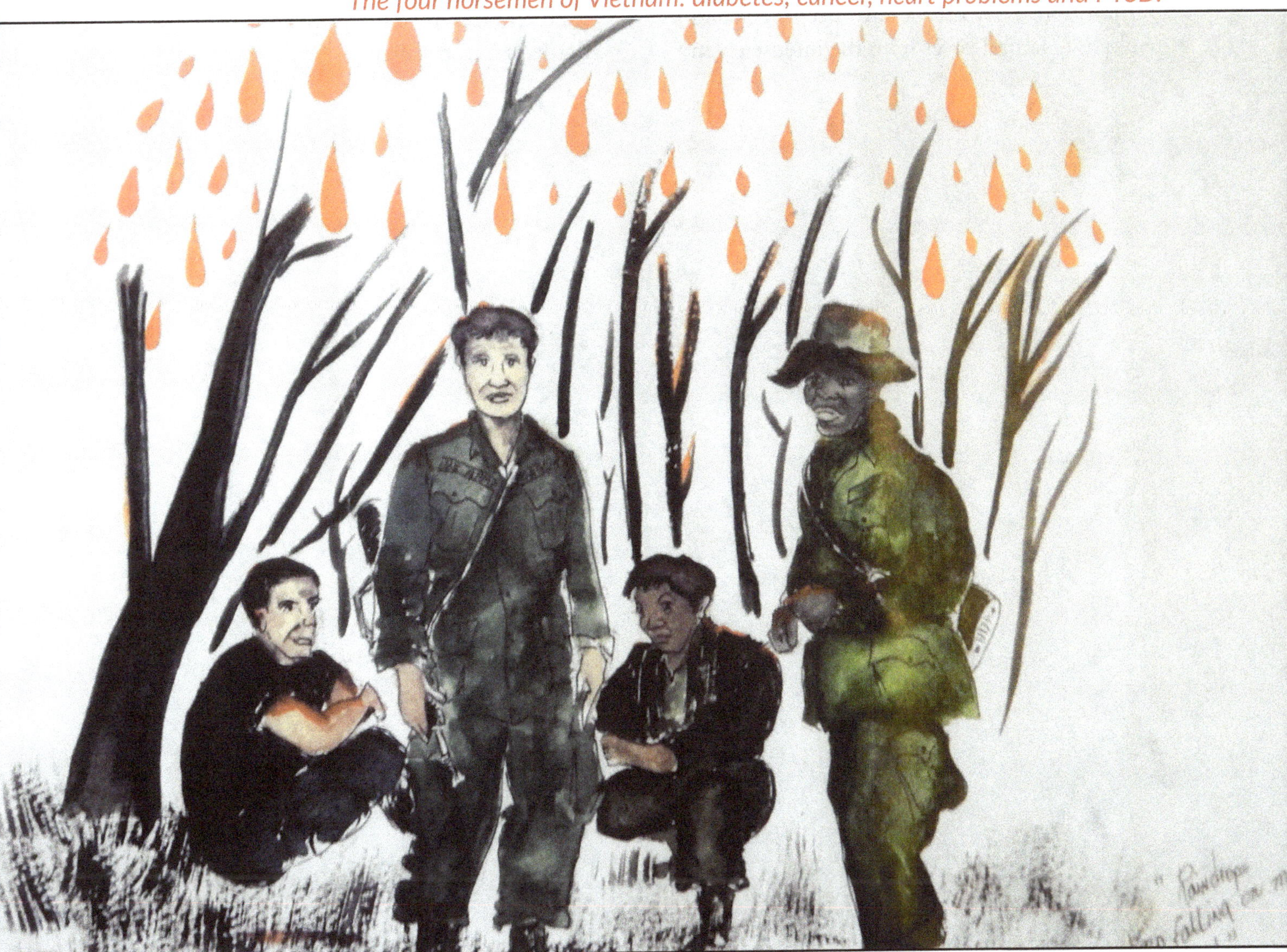

The Battle of Leech Valley

We came out of the hills after weeks of conducting a search and destroy mission with minor enemy contact. As we started setting up a landing zone, my squad was sent to secure the opposite tree-lined side of the LZ. We moved approximately 100 yards up a trail paralleling a creek. As soon as we arrived there, all hell broke loose.

It was the onset of a two-day battle.

More troops were immediately sent to reinforce our position. They used a waist deep creek and its banks as a natural cover from the intense enemy fire. They moved shirtless, some with helmets strapped atop their rucksacks.

Crouched, holding their weapons above water, they were unable to swat the large "elephant" leeches, that infested the creek, off their bodies. Being unaware of the leeches in the stream, the battle raging around us did not scare me as much as the look of horror on their faces and the amount of blood that covered their upper bodies.

I still hear the screams above the gunfire. I'll see their faces until I join those who died at the Battle of Leech Valley.

Giant leeches.

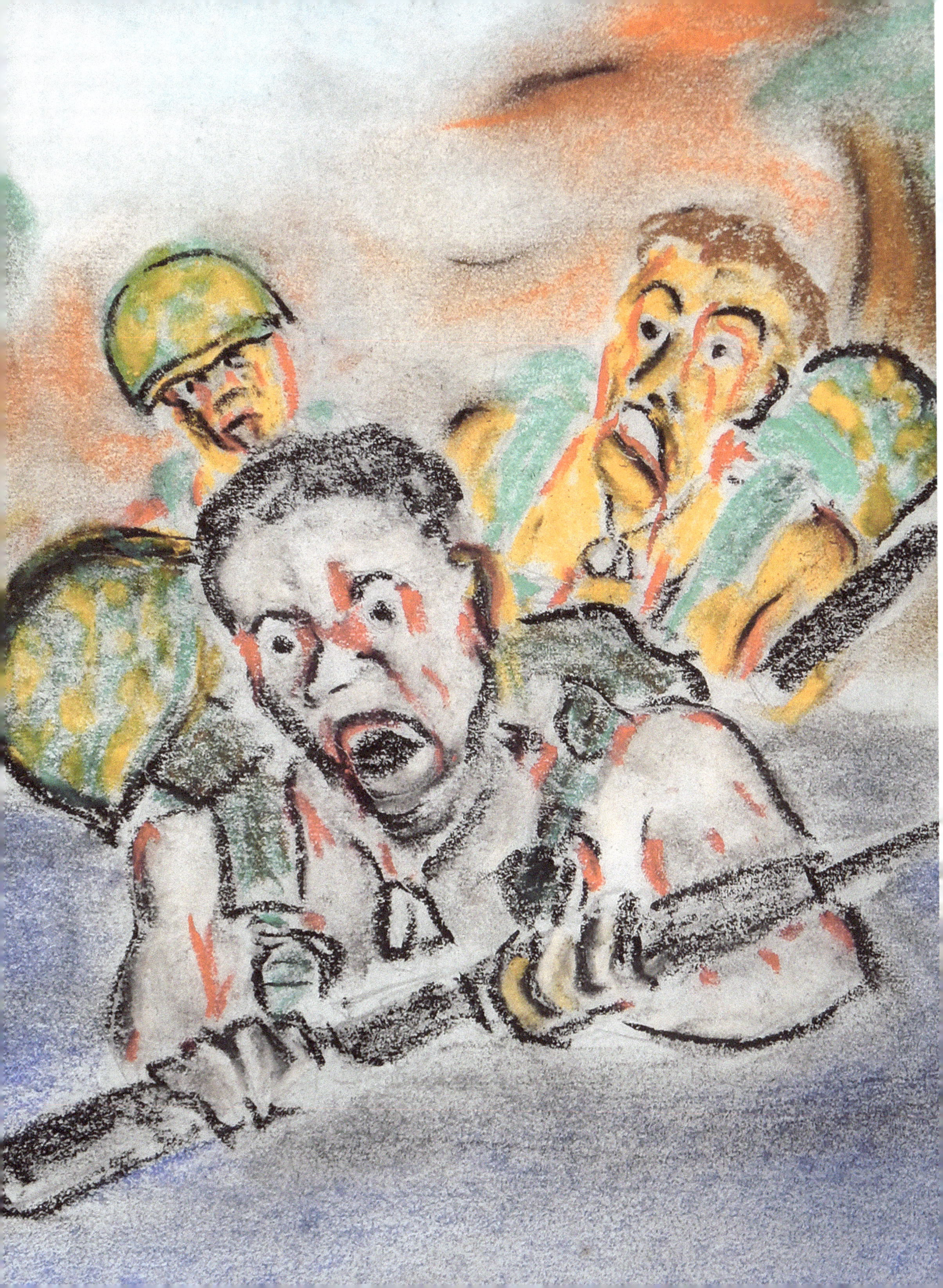

FRIENDLY FIRE

I cannot recollect the exact date, but it was in April 1966, during the Battle of Leech Valley. We were sent to secure a medevac LZ just a short distance, and defilade from the main action at the base of a steep hillside, which we later learned contained a full-service NVA hospital.

They brought the wounded and dead to our location, including a severely wounded Sgt. Caudet who was asking for his brother-in-law, Sgt. Taylor, who showed up shortly afterward to say goodbye to him.

I was watching our gunships come in on their strafing run just above us and to our right. As they banked the chopper port side, the gunner continued firing. I sensed danger and watched the same chopper come in for another run. I was the only one standing.

The medics were working on the wounded. Caudet's brother-in-law was kneeling beside him. I looked right at the gunner, pointed and yelled "he's firing at us," or something to that effect.

When the dust cleared some of the wounded were dead. The medics had laid out Caudet and

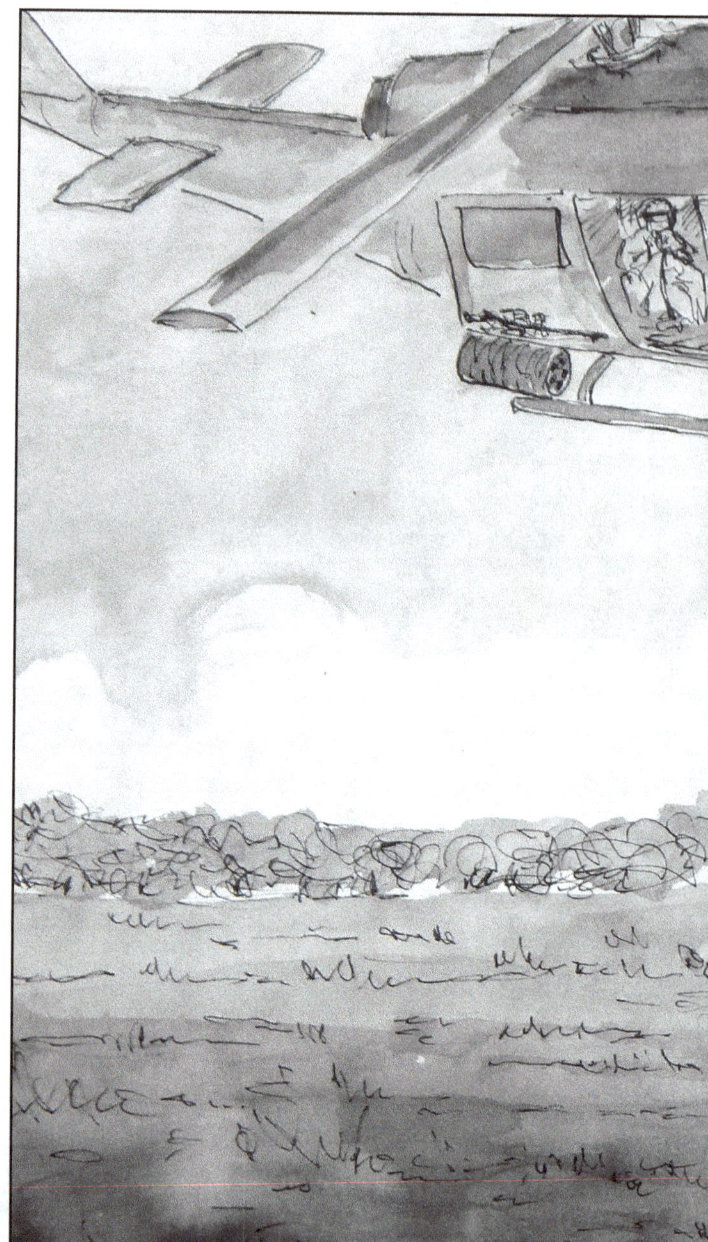

Friendly fire.

his brother-in-law, who were badly wounded, side-by-side.

Only one medic and I were untouched, but the fire from the chopper destroyed my PRC 25 radio transmitter. I'm sure the chopper crew knew what happened because they didn't come in again on the same path, even though it was needed.

We dutifully reported the incident and circumstances. I suspect the information was never passed on. And now I know it was the right thing to do. It was just another incident of friendly fire.

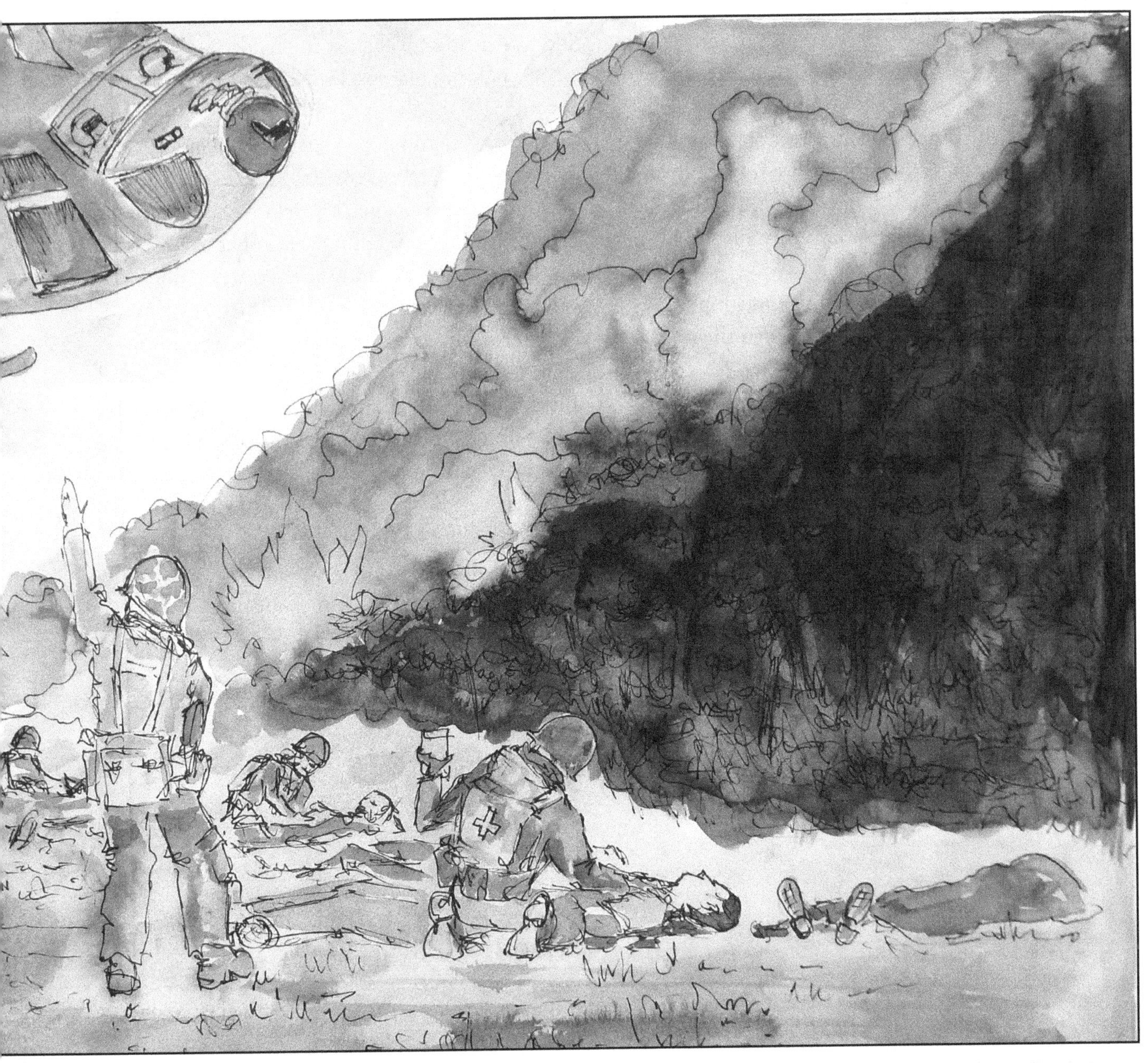

Almost a Deadly Mistake

On this particular moonlit night, my platoon was set up in a triangle formation with my side along a high-speed trail. I was in the middle position with the newest squad member. We were laying in the Savannah grass on a bank above the path. I was beside myself because there seemed to be no noise discipline.

I heard voices coming down the trail. It sounded like English. As they went by, their headgear looked like GI helmets. I couldn't believe these guys were going from one end of the formation to the other to visit. I couldn't take it. I jumped down onto the trail to give somebody a real ass chewing. When I left the bank, I realized my mistake. I was looking at two very surprised North Vietnamese soldiers.

One had a French mat machine gun strapped on his shoulder trying to get it off when the barrel of my M16 hit his chest, as I fired full auto. He just seemed to disappear. The other one had an SKS rifle and fired two shots at my head, blinding me, but I felt my barrel on his torso and fired a burst. He fell instantly. I jumped back on top of the bank landing on top of Pvt. Rodriguez.

I started shaking uncontrollably. For a few seconds, the realization of what I'd just done struck me.

"What the fuck did you do?" I asked myself while feeling my head to see if any part of it was missing.

One of the Vietnamese was not dead, and after a few minutes, he started talking to himself out loud like there was nothing wrong with him. He kept repeating the word *mai* several times in his conversation with someone. I could see his head. He was sitting up against the bank.

By then the platoon leader and sergeant were on my case.

"What did you do? What if they were the point for the larger element?" They yelled.

They had some choice words for me, and I responded in kind, telling them that even if they got by me, they would hear the party going on to our right. I had no respect for either of them.

After a while, the dead man talking got on everyone's nerves, and they insisted that I go and finish the job. By then I felt sorry for the guy, but I had to do it because he was in bad shape. It was a bad night for me too.

After we got back to our base camp a couple of days later, the platoon sergeant left to the rear and did not come back and the platoon lieutenant was relieved for a screw-up on his part. I never saw either again.

I got the shakes.

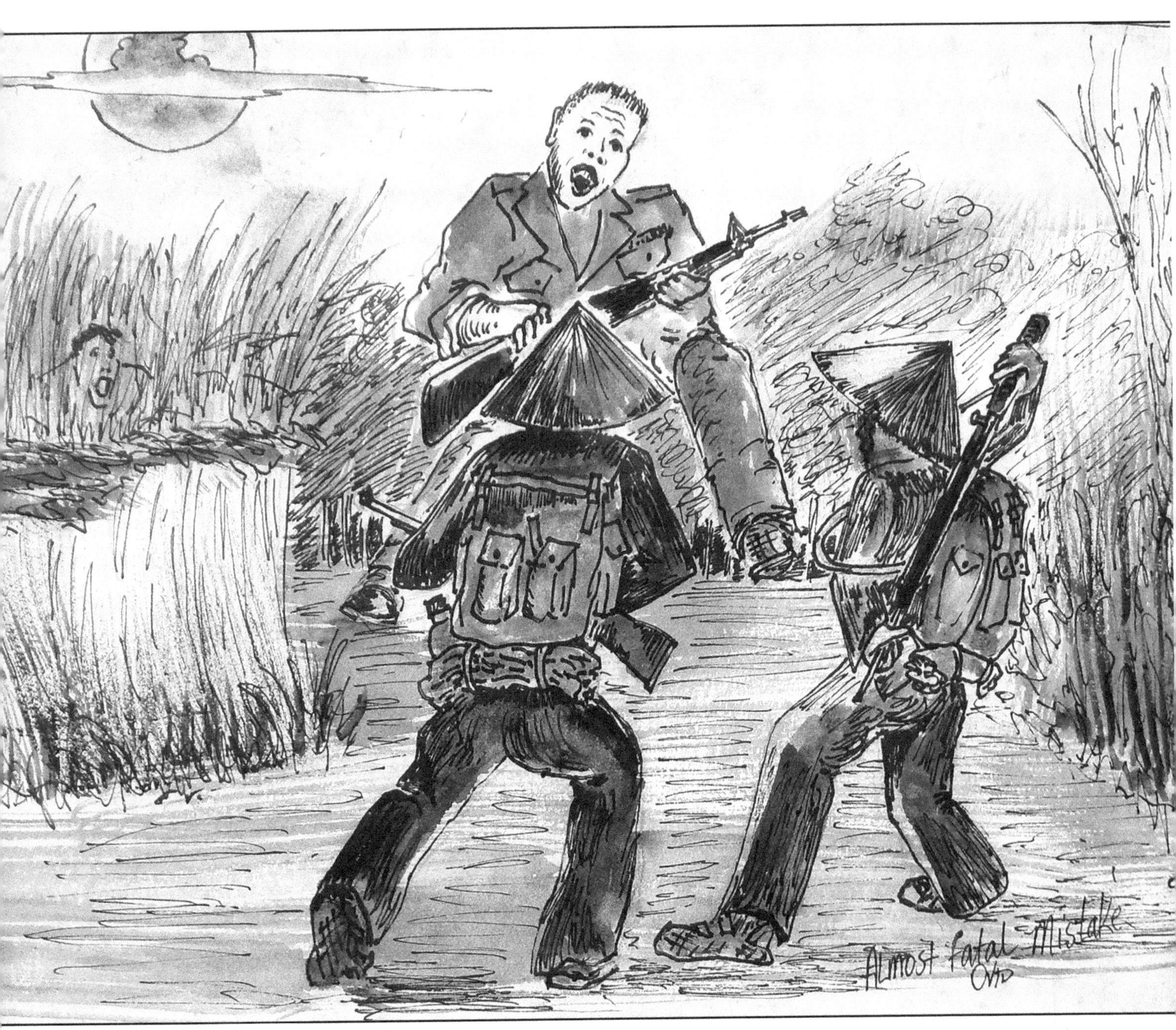

Almost Fatal Mistake
Ovd

TOES

While operating in the Tuy Hoa area, a Free Fire Zone, we took a break from patrol by hiding in a wooded hillside crest. We spotted two VC load-bearers walking along the valley floor trail from our right to left, close to a nearby village. I aimed at the first one, and my M60 gunner spotted the second.

I told the gunner to fire a single shot and then spray the area on my command. Our targets were at about 100 yards. Looking down my weapon, I knew it was not zeroed, so I aimed high above his head. We fired. They dropped their loads and took off towards the opposite side showing no signs of being hit by the automatic fire.

We went down to see what they had dropped. The first Vietnamese had jumped out of his right Ho Chi Minh sandal leaving it right-side up with his big toe and the next toe dangling from the sandal front with just a little splatter of blood. It was like someone had taken a meat cleaver and come down quick and hard, separating the toes from the foot before the owner had a chance to react with pain and blood. We were all amazed and awed at the position of the toes. A couple of guys were laughing almost hysterically.

But they were watching us too, and they dropped a mortar round close to us. We jumped into a dry creek bed for cover. Still laughing while SP/4 Brown did an imitation of a Viet limping into a bar and someone asking why he walked funny. He would say, "Well, I was just walking down this trail…"

After a while, most of us developed a morbid sense of humor.

Two toes less.

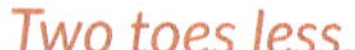

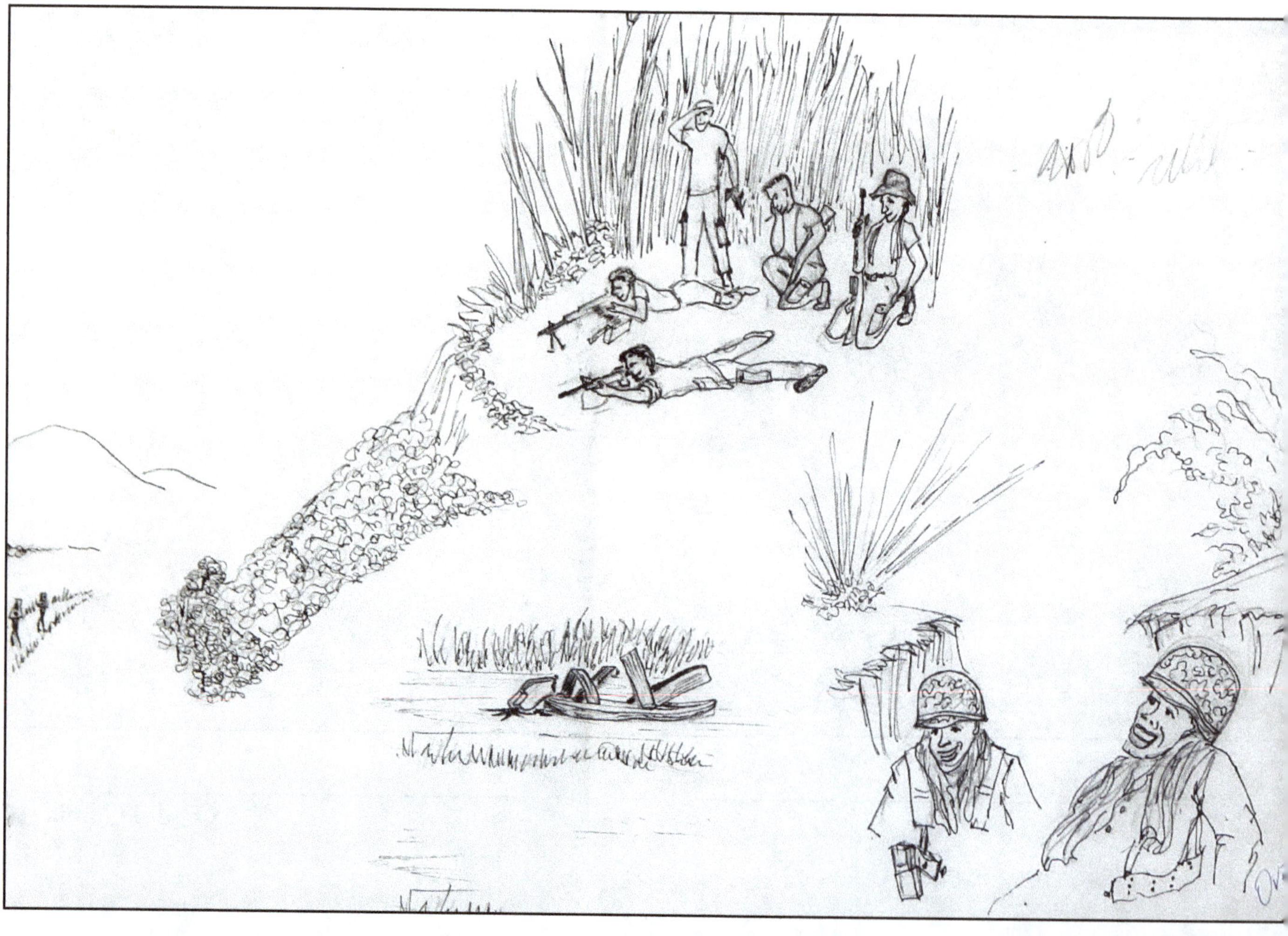

Alas, Poor Yorick

Our company was moving through the jungle during a heavy rainstorm. I was somewhere in the middle of the single file column that was continually stopping due to the terrain. I leaned against the side of the higher ground to rest and saw a human skull caught in some exposed tree roots. I picked it up, was looking at it and noticed the guys around looking at me.

In my best imagined Shakespearean voice, I said, "Alas poor Yorick. I knew him well."

The troops all started laughing. Probably at my heavily accented rendition. But a couple knew from which Shakespearean play it came.

I climbed up a 10-foot high bank and found myself on a cleared flat ground area approximately twenty feet around with branches and tree limbs interwoven to prevent detection from the air. In the center were the ashes of an old campfire. One human skeleton was lying in a fetal position beside the ashes. A second skeleton, missing a skull, was laying on it's back on top of a decomposed nylon hammock. Both had died there by themselves from wounds or illness.

I immediately felt emotionally moved, imagining their loneliness and suffering during the last minutes of their lives. But then I caught myself. If I had found these two alive, I would have no qualm about shooting them, and that was the totality of that reality.

Empathy is short-lived.

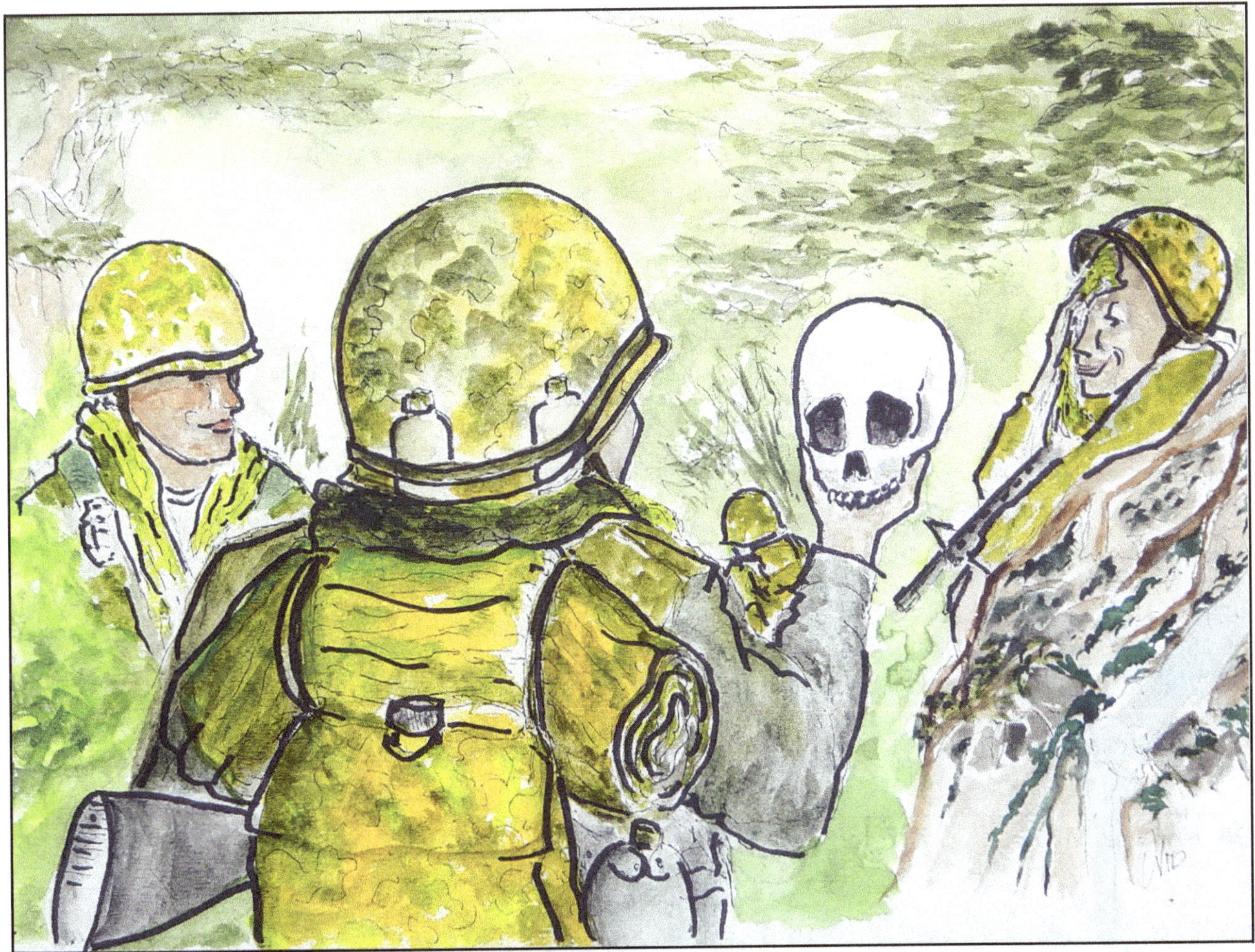

B52 Bomb Blast

In May 1966, around Ban Me Thuot while assessing an arc light strike on a section of the Ho Chi Minh Trail we entered an area within a few hours and came upon an NVA officer who seemed to be sleeping. He was leaning on a tree stump. His pith helmet was tilted over his face.

But it was an eternal sleep.

Upon removing the helmet from the body, we saw his eyes were on his cheeks, hanging from the eye sockets held only by tendrils. Close to and above him was a sight that perplexed me for many years. How could a body wrap itself around a tree? We didn't have time to loiter around. It was check it out and leave.

Forty-one years later, at approximately 8:45 in the morning, December 10, 2007, while laying in

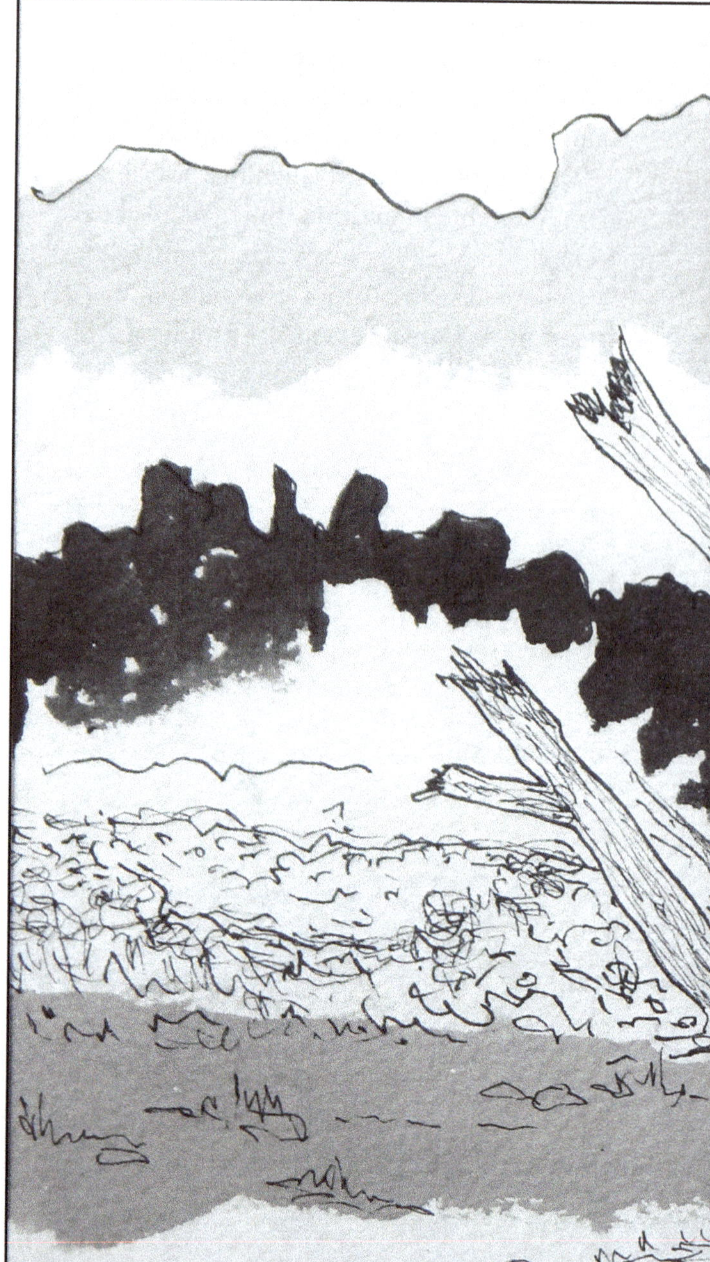

Bad dreams.

bed beside my wife, I solved the mystery that had plagued me since then.

I woke up from a dream that revealed to me how a human body could wrap itself around a tree like a snake. In my dream, I was in the bomb blast area observing and feeling the power of the bomb. I saw the body flying through the air, hit a tree at the midsection and wrap itself around. I jumped out of bed and started drawing.

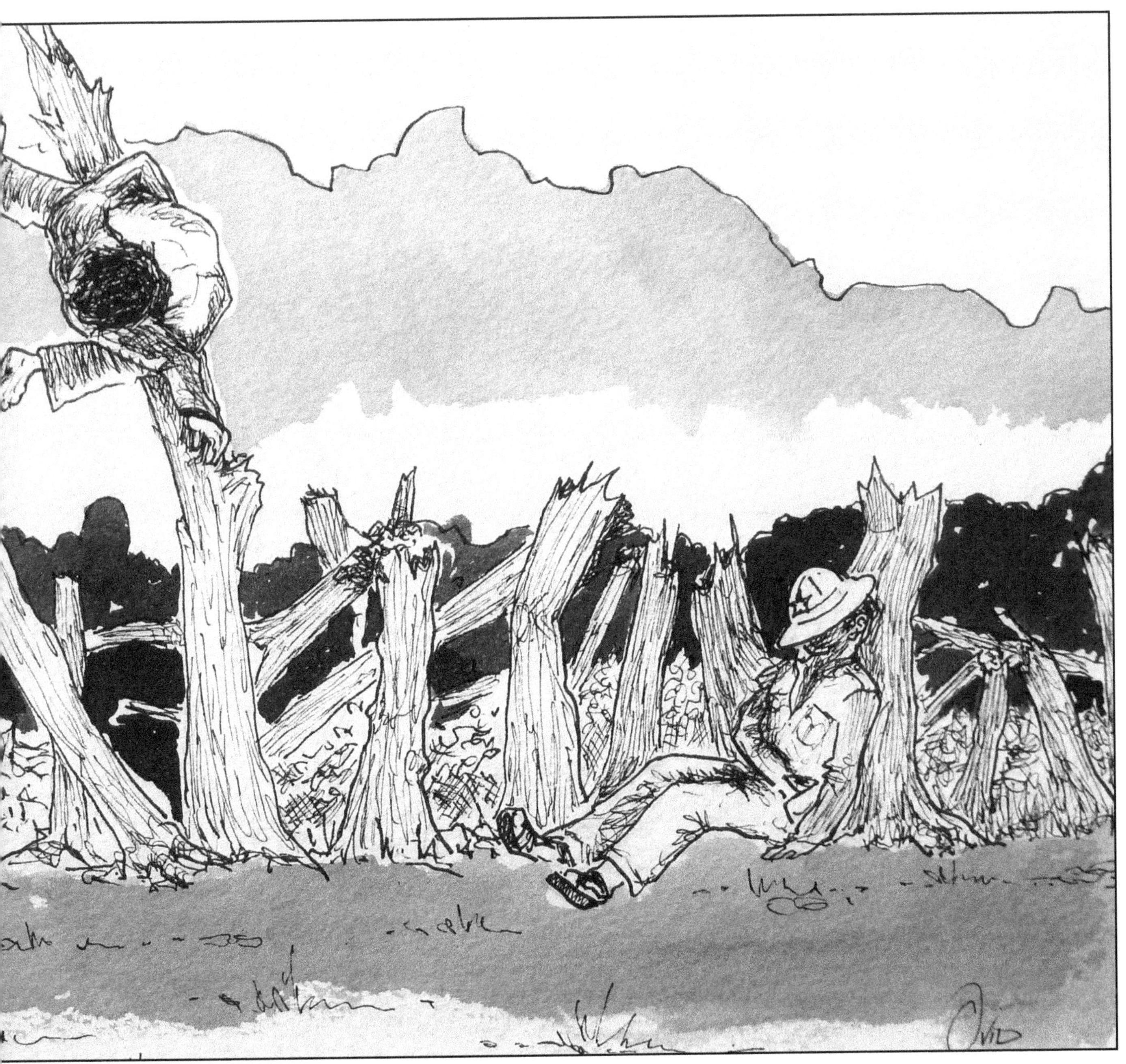

No Jungle Experts

S ometime in May 1967, our unit was flanking a retreating North Vietnam Army unit who were trying desperately to make it across to a haven in the nearby South Vietnam-Cambodian border.

Because of our proximity and repeated contacts with the enemy, I was walking point and Sgt.

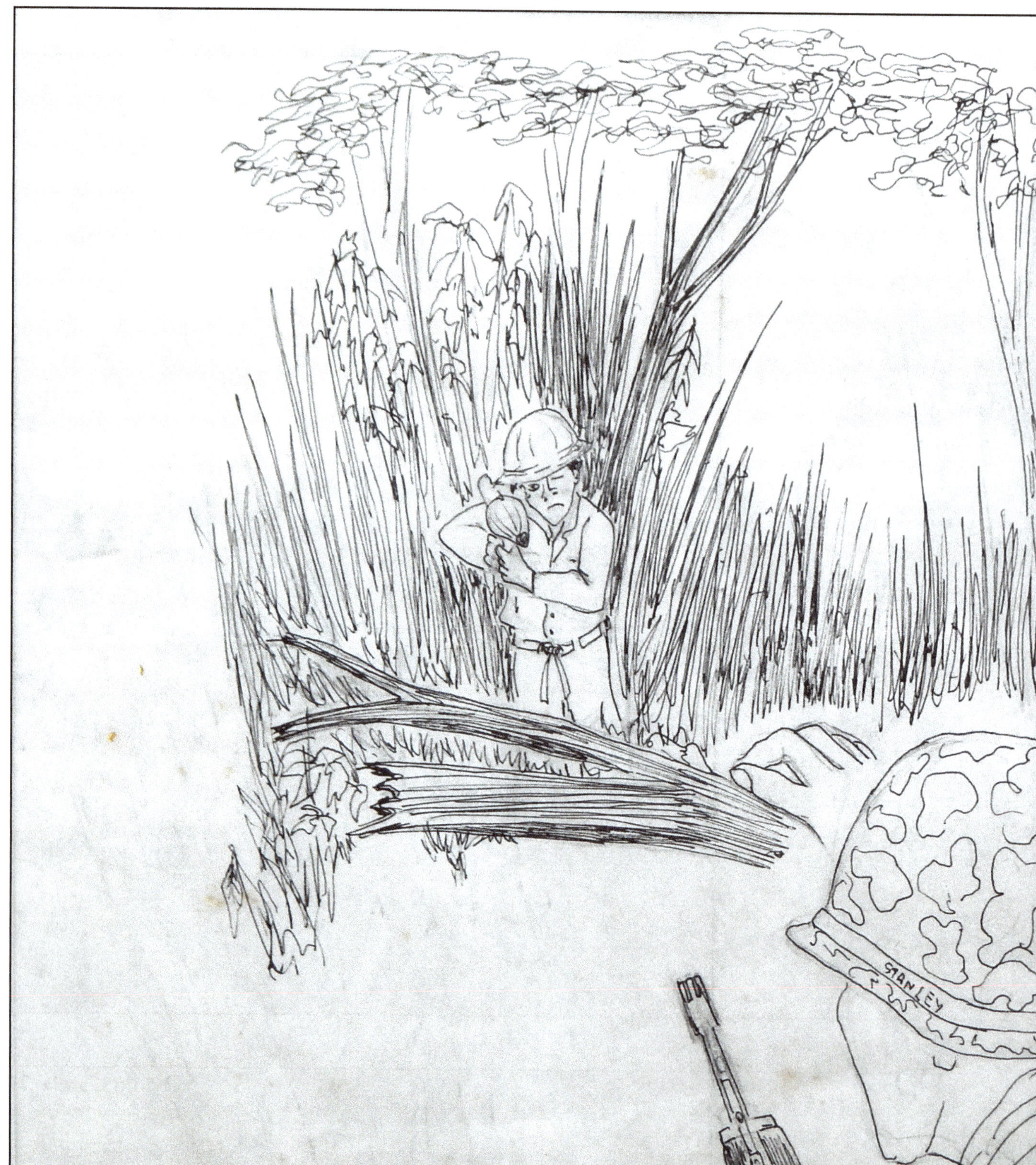

Stanley was my backup. As we entered a small clearing, Sgt. Stanley told me to stop. I turned and quickly followed his line of sight and rifle

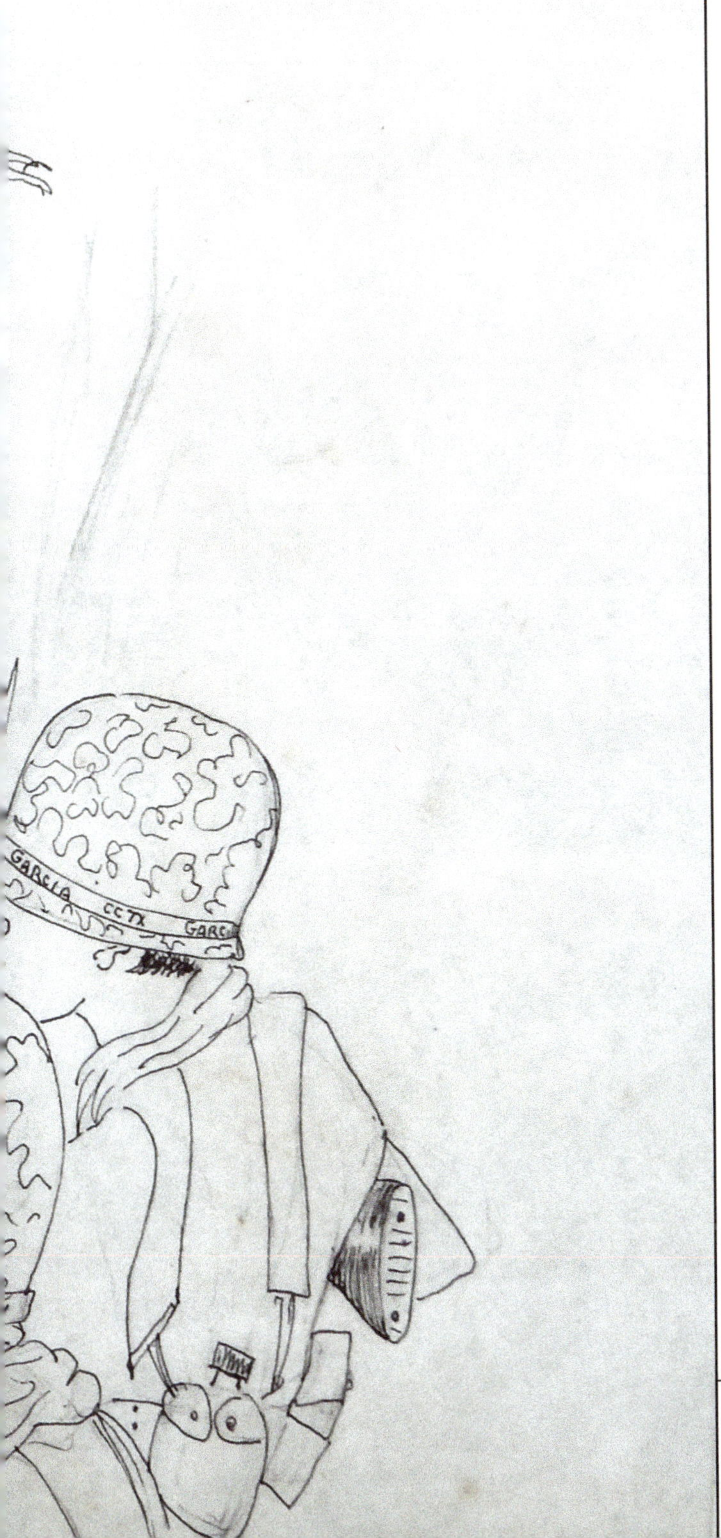

barrel to an enemy soldier about 20-feet away on the other side of the clearing. He was standing behind some logs pointing an RPG (rocket-propelled grenade) our way.

We both had our weapons pointed at him and shouted: "dung lo" which we thought meant surrender in Vietnamese, but we found out later that depending on the voice inflection it can mean a number of things. Still, he must have understood what we meant for he slowly laid the RPG down and raised both arms.

Sgt. Stanley and I gave him food, water, and a cigarette before our scout, an old, wily veteran of a lot of warfare, dating back to the French, came up to question him. Through our scout, we found out that he was 19-years-old, from North Vietnam and had crossed the border into the South not too long before. He had gotten separated from his unit a couple of days back. He had not eaten or drunk water since then. He was suffering from dysentery, malaria and starving.

I had noticed that our Kit Carson (our name for local scouts) carried on his pack suspenders a coil of wire with worn wooden handles on each end. I had never seen a garrote in use before. After a short period of questioning and a look of utter disgust, the scout looped the wire around the prisoner's head and started tightening.

Sgt. Stanley and I had to continue on and never saw the end result. Sgt. Stanley commented that the NVA were generally referred to as jungle experts by the news services, but that prisoner knew less about the jungle than we did.

We both agreed that the only jungle experts were the monkeys, and they too got killed now and then.

A matter of semantics.

TREE OF LIFE

While on patrol in the highlands, we came into an area infested with elephant leeches. The big black ones. After the first night, S/P4 Gallant came to where I was laying and said with a trembling voice, "Sarge, look at this."

His look and hands directed me to his crotch.

His pants were torn as most were in that area because of active stretching. When we went back to an rear area after an operation, we regrouped and refitted ourselves with fresh fatigues that hadn't belonged to us and considered ourselves lucky to get the right size. The underwear didn't belong to us either so we passed on underwear.

I looked at his penis hanging outside his pants, and it was like looking at a type of blood sausage; it was reddish purple and just as big. It was dripping blood which had soaked up the front of his pants. I must have said, "Jesus!" or "Oh, shit!" That and the look on my face, and that of the rest of the squad sent him into shock.

It was worse than looking at any wound. It is a man's most important appendage. Gallant was no rookie, and he had comported himself well in other situations, but he was just scared shitless. And it was hard to keep from looking at it.

I got on the radio to our CO and asked for a medevac and told him I had an unconscious man who was on the verge of becoming a casualty from an unknown source. There was a chopper in the air near us, and within thirty minutes it picked Gallant up. Of course, all of us thought he was going to lose his whacker. Someone even said, "Maybe it won't be so bad being a girl. He's not a bad looking guy, slim, tall and blond."

A few hours later, I got a call saying it was a leech that had crawled into his penis orifice.

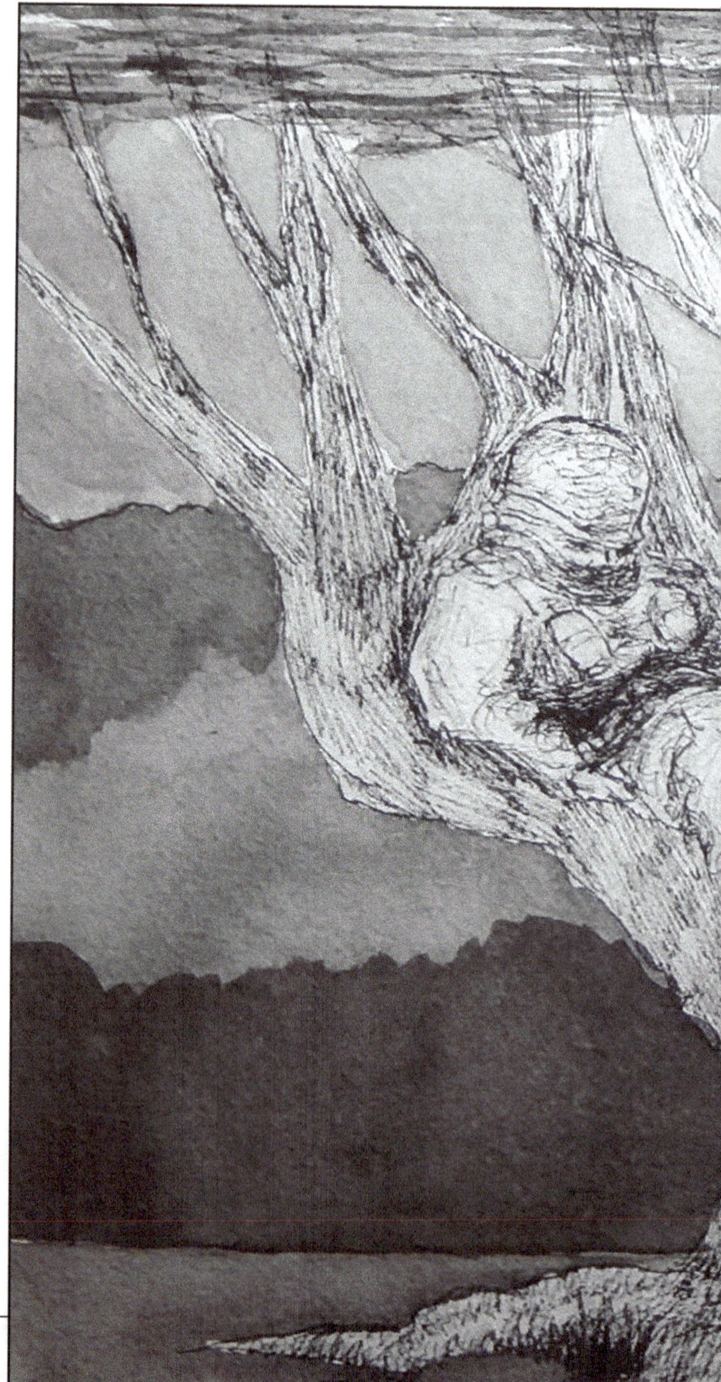

Not the Disney World tree.

It had stayed there sucking blood. But Gallant would be okay.

We were told to cover our holes because the leeches will crawl into any of them. That evening, before dark, we started looking for a large enough, suitable tree. Nobody was going to sleep on the ground. We spent that whole night perched like birds on that tree. Even then, I woke up gagging on blood. I had one on the roof of my mouth!

Gallant rejoined us two weeks later with a new appreciation for his pecker. I never forgot his name because of this incident.

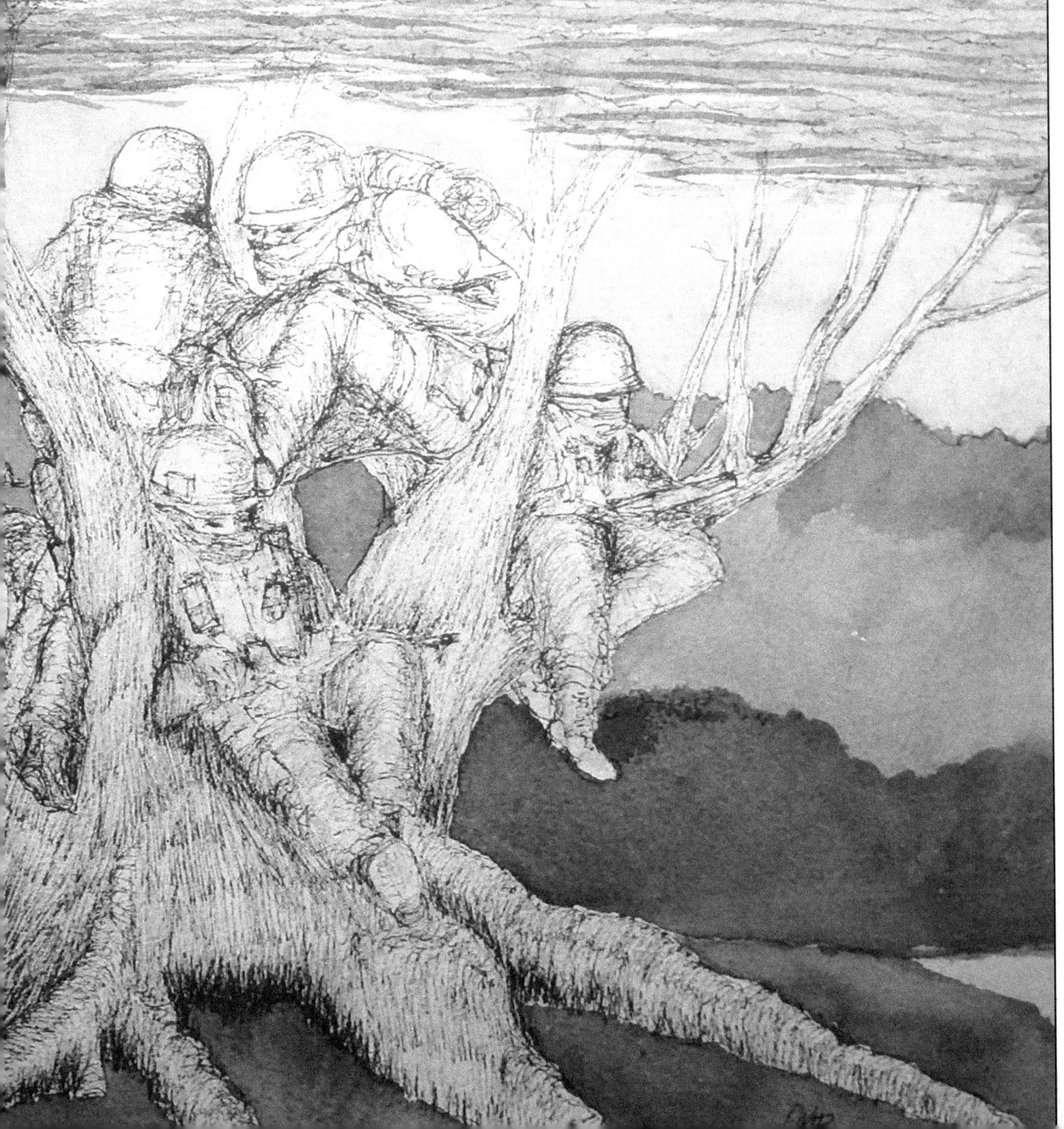

Punji Stakes

During an operation in the Phan Tiet area in May 1966, about five of us were sent up a trail to check it out while our Company stood down and regrouped. I took the lead point with SFC Williams backing me up and three others behind. Before I realized it, I was standing inside the perimeter of a well-hidden NVA camp. It blended in with all the surround-

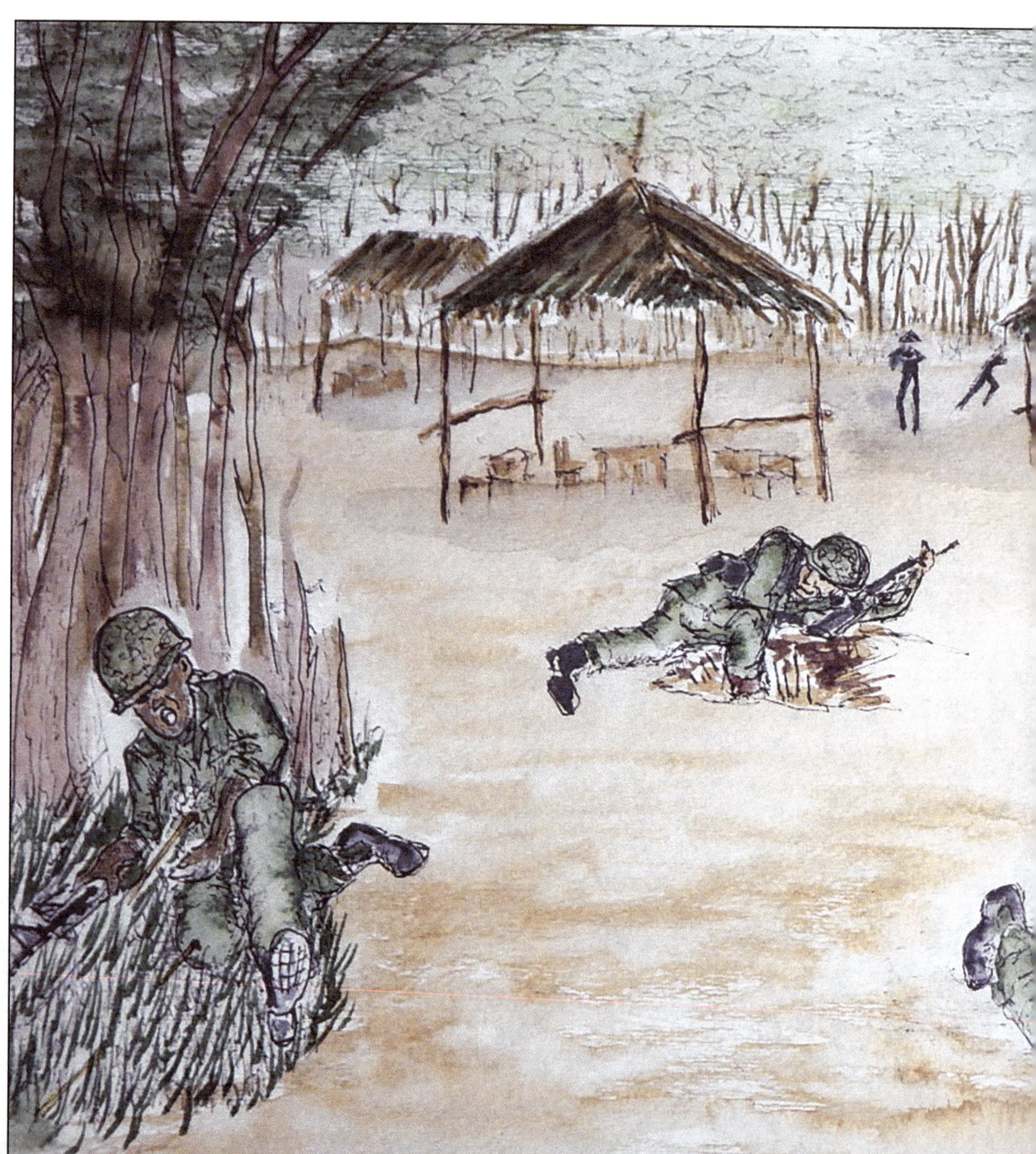

ings perfectly. My eyes and mind were still trying to talk to each other when I saw movement
at the other end and made out one NVA fixing
to fire at me.

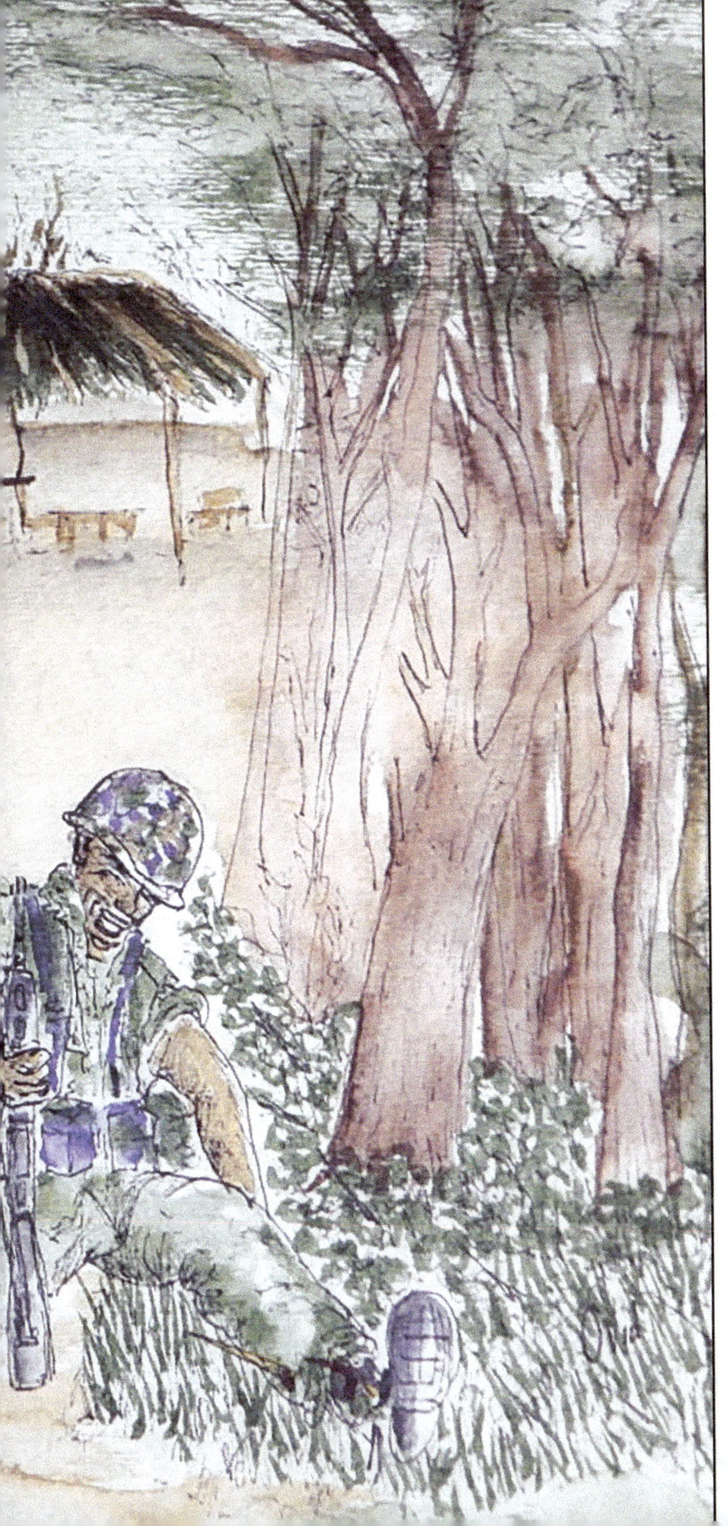

I ran forward towards cover nearby, but I
stepped on the edge of a well concealed, deep
punji pit. Luckily only my right foot slid in, but
a human feces-encrusted stake went all the way
through my calf.

I was lucky. When the NVA fired at us, SFC
Williams, who was behind me, jumped to his
right. He landed to the right of the trail and
drove two stakes into his foot and ankle. A third
man dove to the side of the path and impaled
himself with several stakes. The worst one went
into his stomach.

The stakes were extremely sharp and able
to penetrate webbing and leather easily. They
went into flesh like a hot knife through butter.
Initially, you didn't feel it, but within a few
minutes, there was an immense pain. They were
smeared with feces and placed along trails where
sometimes they were impossible to detect until
you fell on one.

DAK TO

On June 6, 1966, my Company started on an operation, leaving a group of us behind. Most of the men in this group were returning to the U.S. after completion of their tour in South Vietnam. Some were recovering from wounds or illnesses.

I was supposed to leave the next day on R&R, one week out of the country for rest and recuperation, which all military personnel assigned to S. Vietnam received during their one year tour. But by that evening, as we sat around the TOC listening to our radios, we heard our Company come under heavy fire. From all the screaming and yelling, we could tell it was bad. The casualty reports began to come in. So some of us started loading up ammo and grenades. The call for volunteers came, and we flew out to an LZ where our Company was reorganizing after heavy losses.

We formed a relief force to find my platoon, which had been moving separately from the Company. We located them, made contact with the survivors and later found the rest still lying in the kill zone. My platoon had walked right into an NVA defensive line with machine gun positions with fields of fire set up by an enemy that had been fighting all their lives.

The two point-men, my new platoon Sergeant Hannah, a Korean War veteran with only two weeks in Viet Nam, and a brand new Lieutenant who had just joined us a week before and his RTO were out front and never had a chance.

I lucked out, again.

I had to identify the bodies where they fell, as I was the only one who knew them. The butchery of forty or fifty rounds in each of them horrified me. These were men I had just talked

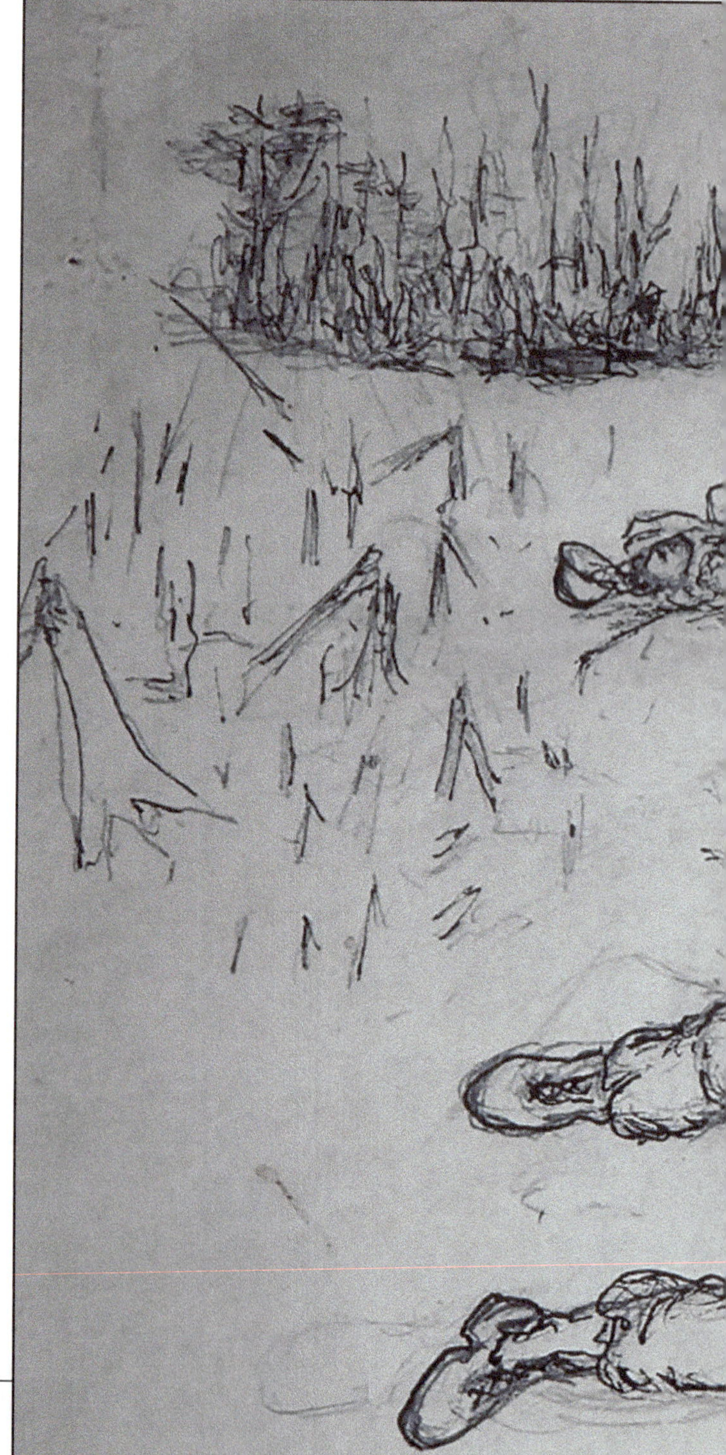

and laughed with the day before. Now they were gone. There were only five survivors.

I felt guilty because I had not been there and, at the same time, glad that I wasn't because they would have killed me too. Was it fate, destiny, or some karma?

I have no choice but to believe in something greater than myself.

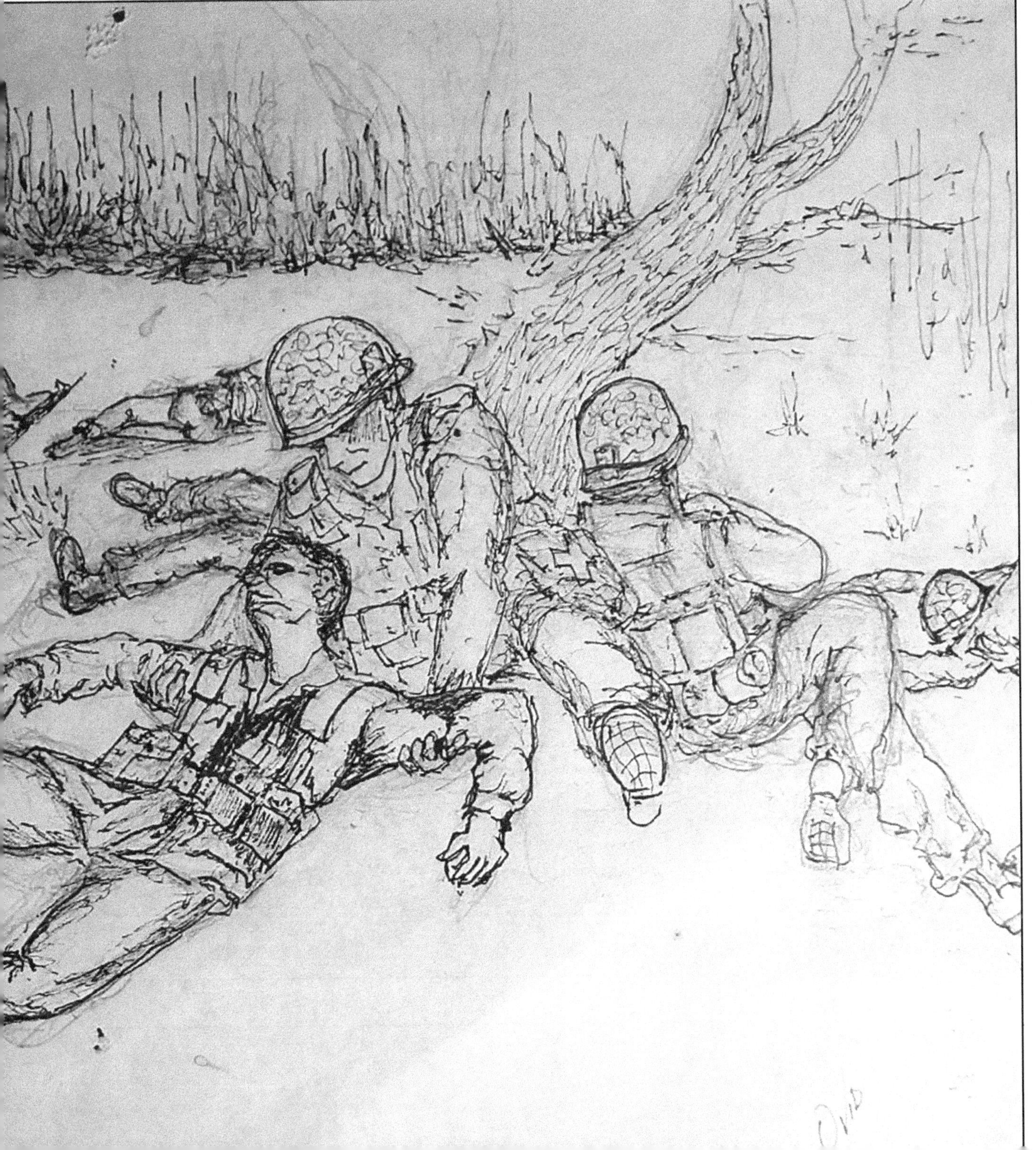

THE STORM

I can't remember the date, but it was one of the most memorable and miserable nights in my life, but Mother Nature administered this punishment. We were along the coast in the II Corps area north of Saigon. Our Company was informed to batten down because we were to be hit by a typhoon, and hit we were. I saw some guys that tied themselves to trees.

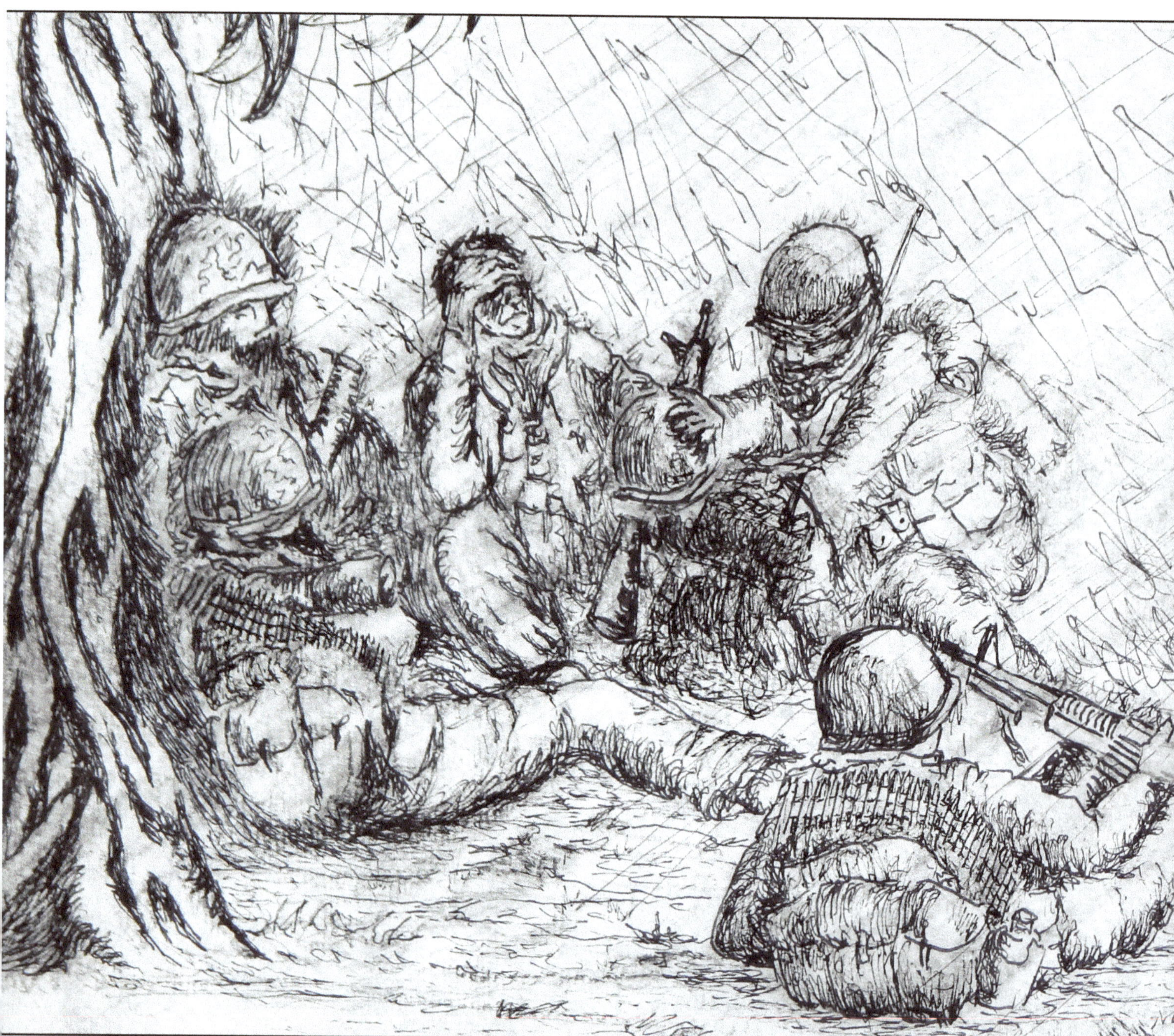

We had no protection against the rain and wind. Thank God, there was no heavy debris flying except for leaves and branches. It was impossible to do anything but just sit.

Through that night I had many misgivings about my choice of career. I could be in a nice and cozy bed with my wife. I could have gone to college and become a lawyer. I could be in a thousand other places besides here!

But like all bad things, it passed. We were all miserable, but no one was hurt.

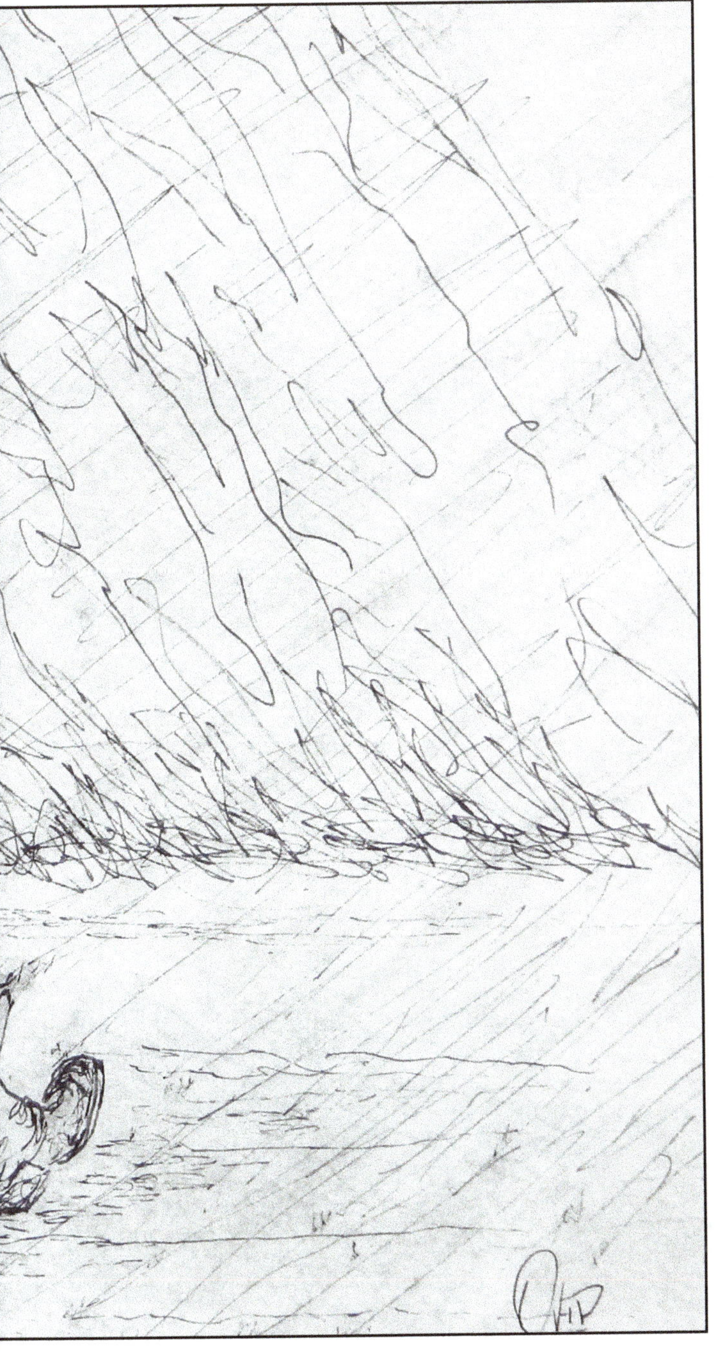

A miserable night.

The Rat Who Bit Me

Sometime in January 1971, after operating for several days in river bottom land, always wet, I decided that I would take my boots off that night and give my feet an airing, no matter what.

One night, before sunrise, a tug on my left toe woke me up. In front of me was the biggest river rat I had ever seen, and he had my big toe in his mouth.

At that instant, he bit down on my toe, right through the nail. My M-16 was laying at my side.

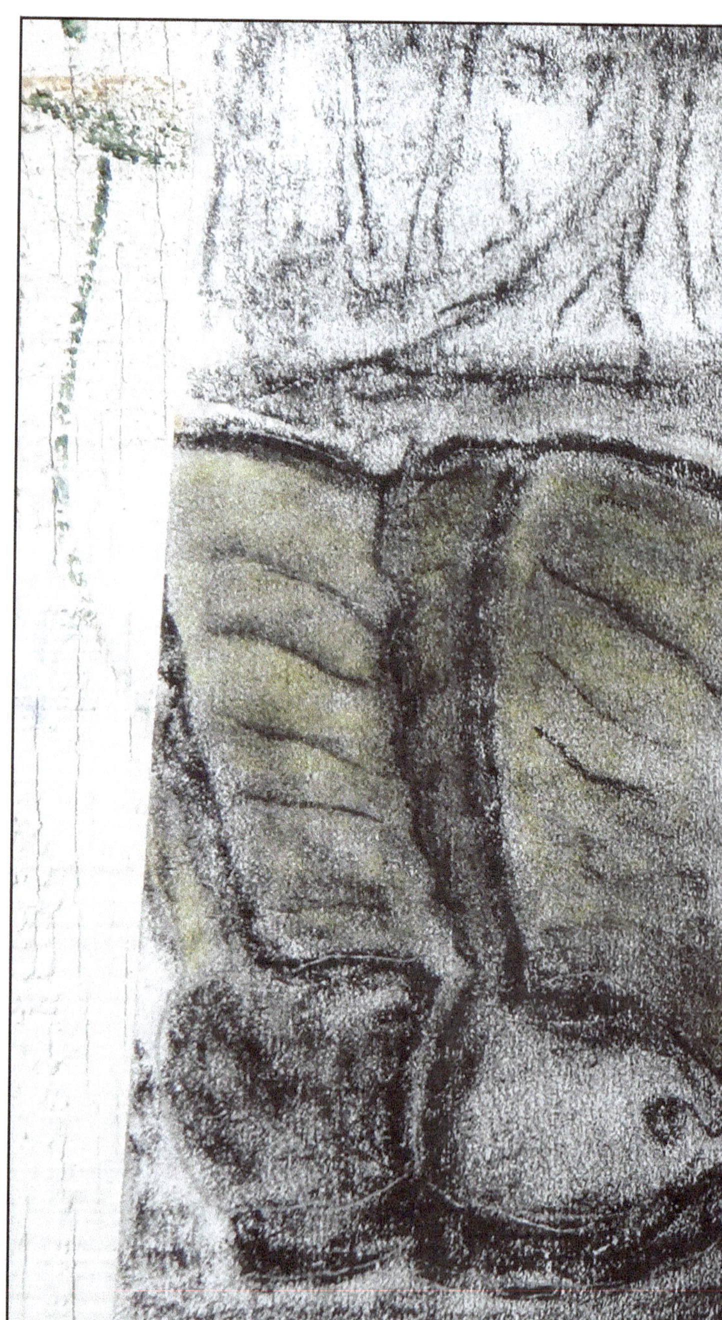

An abrupt wake up call.

It was off safe and set on full automatic. I picked it up and fired a full burst at the rat.

Luckily I didn't hit him; I didn't blow my foot off, either. Thank God I didn't shoot the two guys on the listening post about 50 yards directly in front of me.

The pain from the rat bite was minor compared to the series of rabies treatment shots that followed.

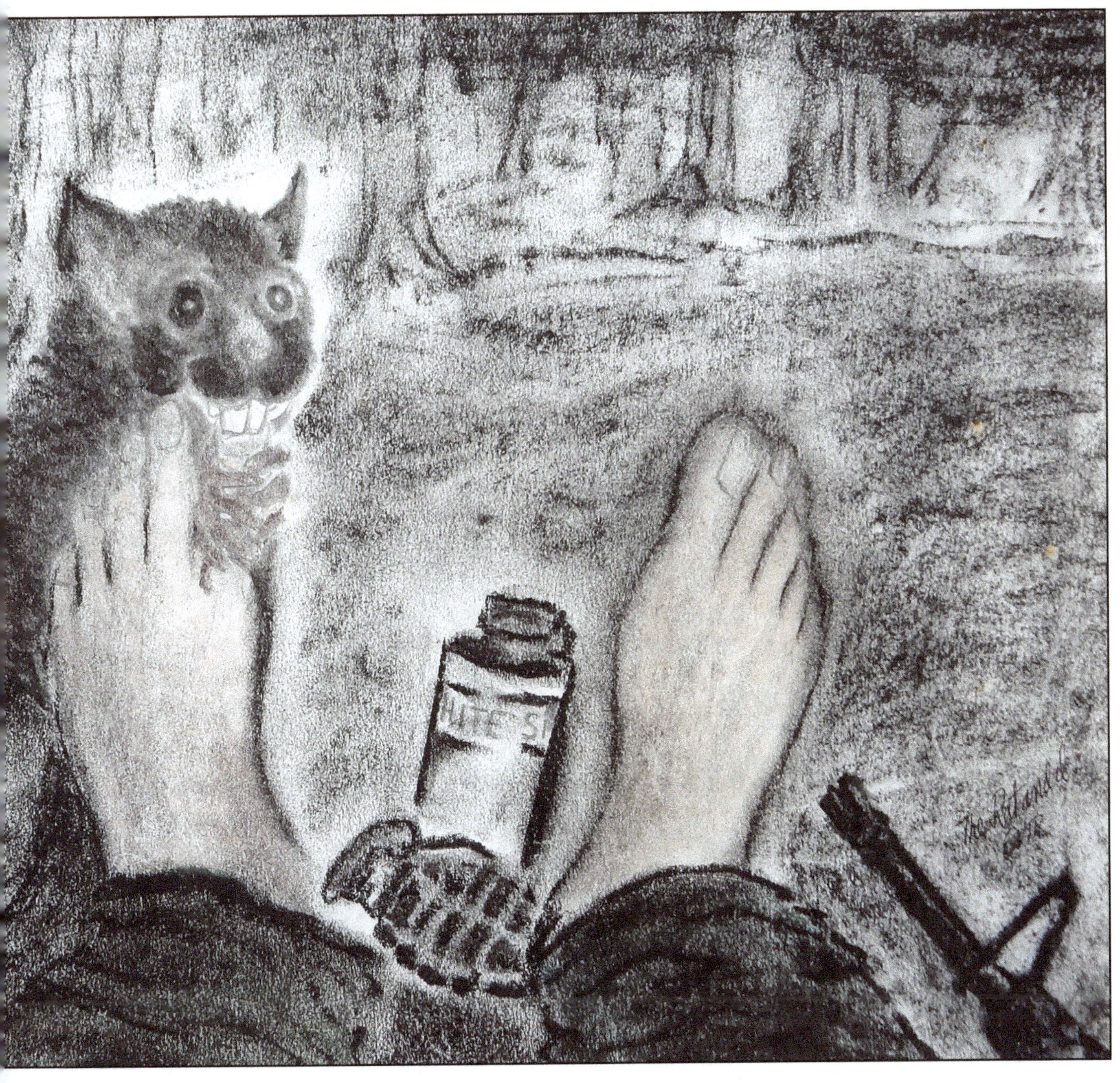

Green Chicharrones

In February 1971, on a Recon Patrol somewhere in Vietnam, we came upon an NVA resupply camp ideally situated in a draw between two mountains with running water and thick overhead tree canopy to prevent it from being spotted from the air. It blended so well with the jungle that we were in it before we realized where we were.

The enemy troops ran before we could get some good shots off. They left everything behind,

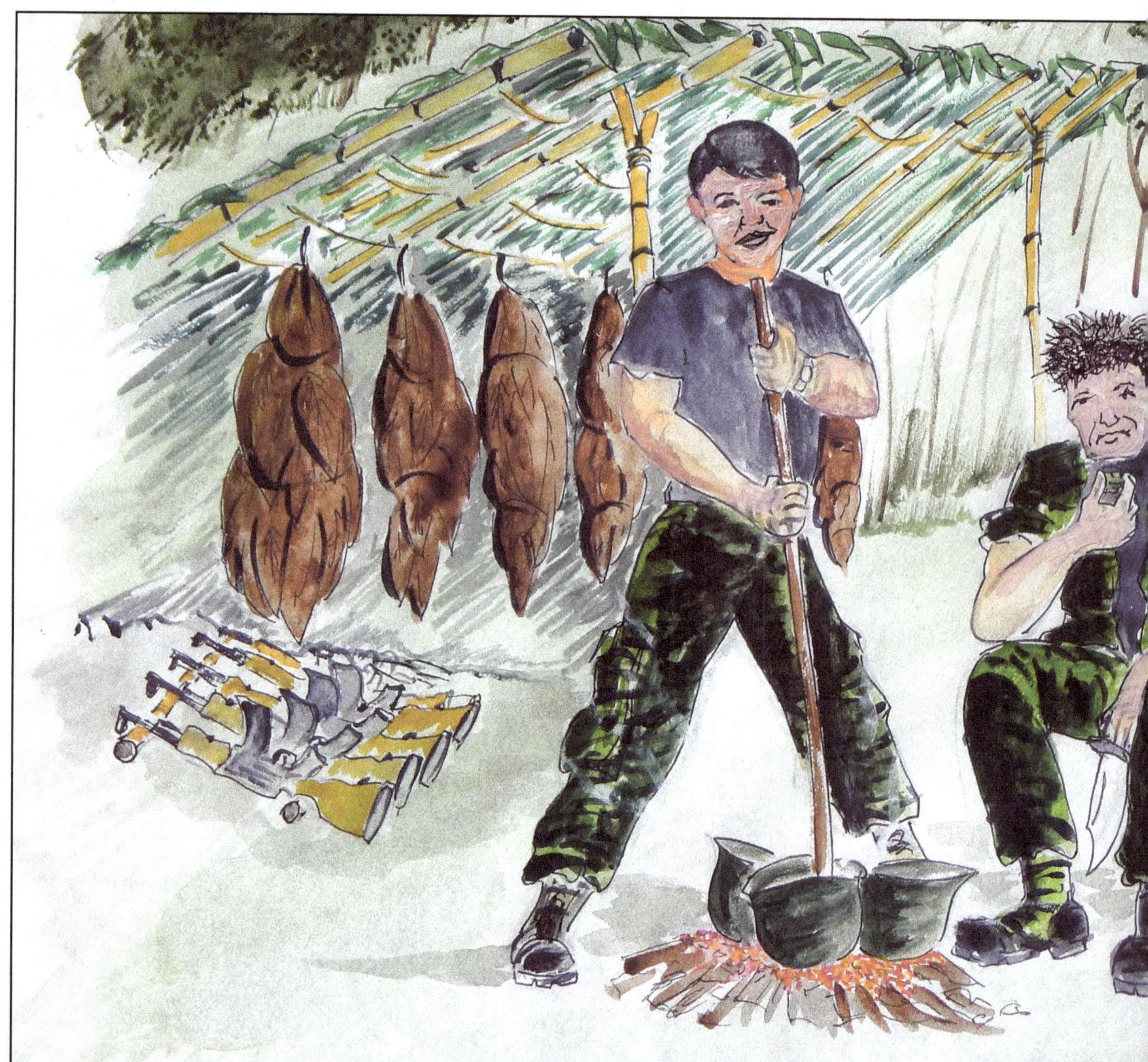

including their stacked weapons, cooking pots over a fire, and a pig they were in the process of slaughtering on a bamboo table.

After we secured the camp and while waiting for the nearby rifle company to secure the area,

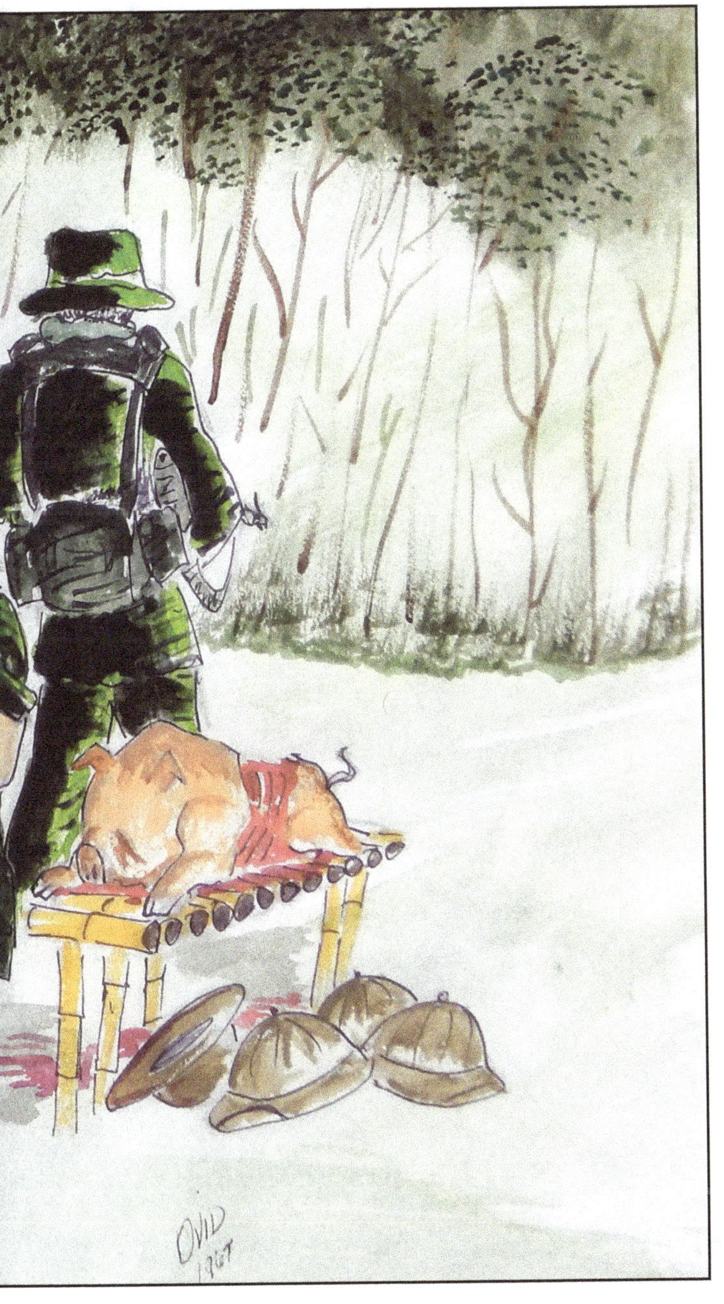

Fine jungle cuisine.

I spied a very fresh pig carcass and remembered the *chicharrones* my grandfather cooked in a black kettle, called a *paila*, over an open fire. He ladled out those delicious chunks of meat consisting of pigskin, lard, and a thin strip of meat. I started reminiscing out loud to Sergeant Pineau, a Louisiana Cajun, who, through "wows" exclaimed, "Oh man, that's the way we make them back home. Let's get it on!"

I told Pineau to start cutting the pig while I stripped three helmets down to steel pots, put them directly on the fire and poured some water in to begin the cooking process. Then Pineau put the chunks of meat in the helmets. Other members of our unit were all smiles in anticipation as I raved about the *chicharrones* and the delicious morsels that would soon be forthcoming. Pineau and I were just beside ourselves, giggling like little kids. We were used to eating C-rations and MREs (meals ready to eat) five days straight.

Unfortunately, the paint on the outside of the helmet started to turn black. The mixture began to bubble, and before long, our *chicharrones* started turning green from the paint color on the inside of the helmet. The other troopers heard me mutter, "Oh shit, they're turning green."

They started breaking out their MREs.

Pineau and I were committed to eating *chicharrones* until we tasted the first and only batch. We could die of many things, but decided it wouldn't be from eating green *chicharrones*.

Stand Down

Every four to five days, the troops in the field were resupplied or brought back to their Base Camps for rest and resupply. Besides carrying all our earthly possessions on our back, we also carried at least a load of ammo plus grenades, smokes and fragmentation, a claymore mine and, last but not least, a chunk of C-4 plastic explosive meant for clearing a Loading Zone in an emergency, but more often used for cooking and hot coffee.

Unfortunately, during the periods that they assigned me to the 173rd and 101st, both units

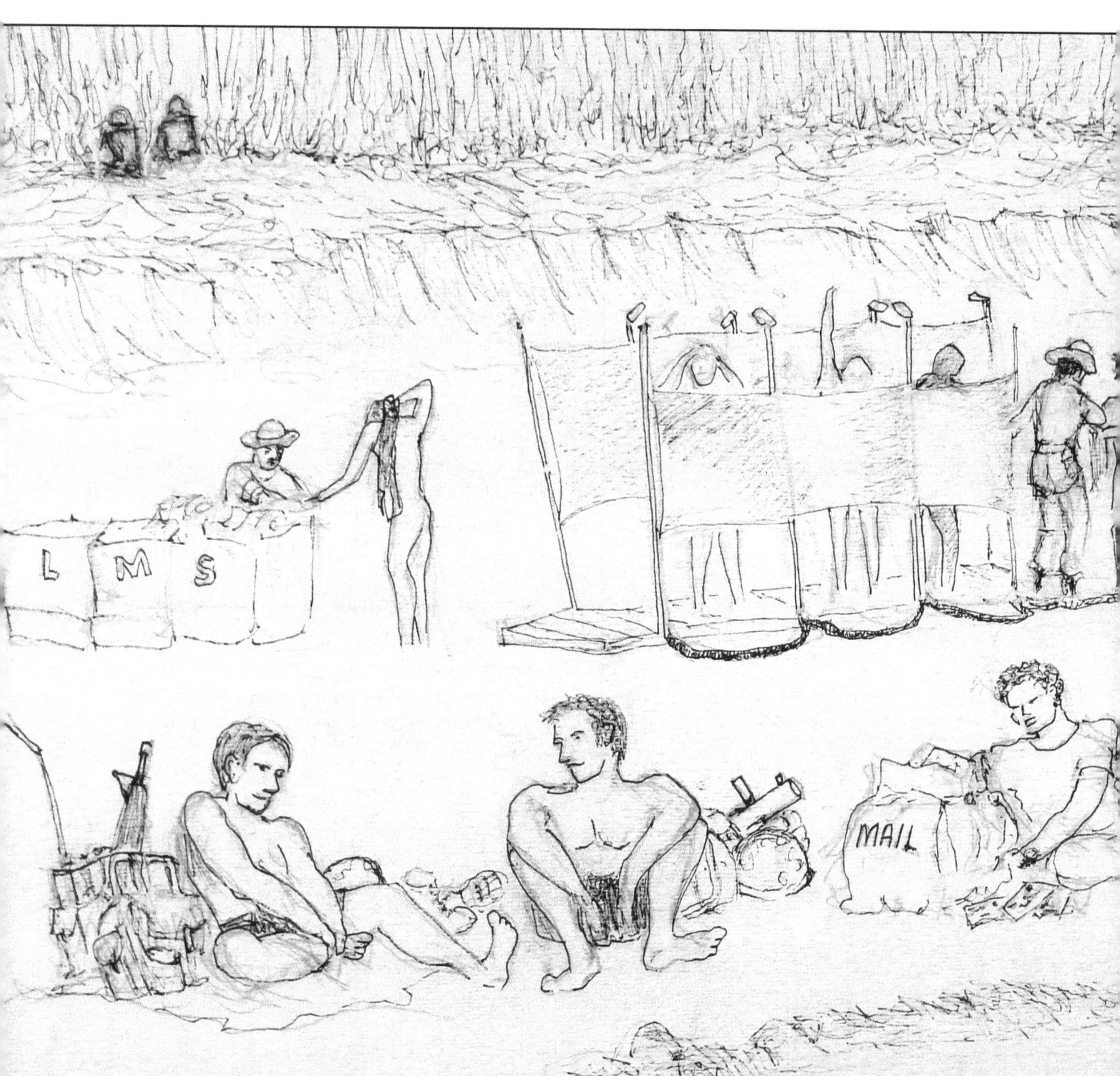

lived in the field and went from one operation
to the next and only occasionally got a few days
pulling security for an artillery unit. It felt like
a rest area to us because they were set up in a
fortified position with concertina wire, giving the
illusion of safety, enabling us to get more sleep

unless our big guns were firing. We were also able
to take off our backpacks for a few days.

The artillery units usually had a helipad in
the center and choppers were coming and going,
so that meant at least one hot meal a day. A
supply and support unit flew into a secured area,
preferably with a water source. In the field, we
bathed when we crossed a river and got wet.

A shower consisted of wooden planks for
the floor, a canvas around shower poles for
privacy, and gas generators pumping water. At
the entrance, you got a bar of soap and at the
exit a towel. Then you proceeded to the various
hampers where you got used clean clothes that
corresponded to your size. No underwear as no
one wanted to wear somebody else's. We got a hot
meal which was a misnomer; it just didn't come
from a can or a bag.

The most important event was mail call when
everything was forgotten, and you could mentally
transport yourself back home and visualize your
loved ones. The ones who were lucky enough to
receive goodies, sweets or jerky, shared them with
their brothers-in-arms with no thought of race,
creed, or political beliefs because they had your
back. At night you laid with each other belly-to-
belly or back-to-back as we slept. We joked about
how close to each other we slept, but I don't
think we have ever slept that close to anyone ever
again in our lives.

The shared camaraderie is one that field
soldiers have experienced since Day One.

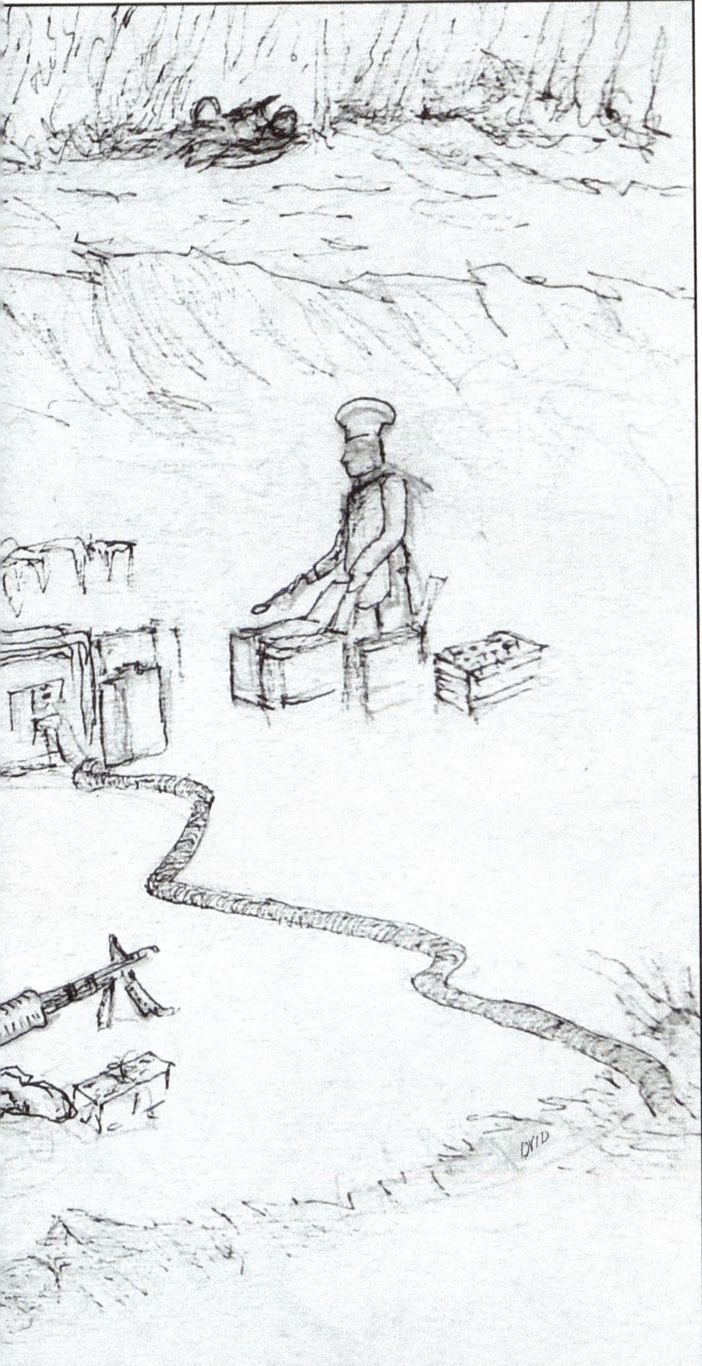

Field resupply.

War Dogs

I love dogs, always have and always will. In 1971 I was a platoon sergeant and Company Field First. The most senior NCO in the field. A dog and handler came in on a resupply helicopter for our company's use as needed. When I welcomed him into our Company, I informed him that there was a lot of enemy activity in our area. I sensed that this was a scared young man, but who could blame him.

Everyone knew that our days in Vietnam were numbered and no one wanted to be the last to die in this "debacle" as Paul Harvey called this mess.

That evening, the handler claimed that the dog might not be up to par for trips outside the perimeter, this being his first contact with all the troops here.

"Hey," I said to myself, "he's the dog expert, we're not."

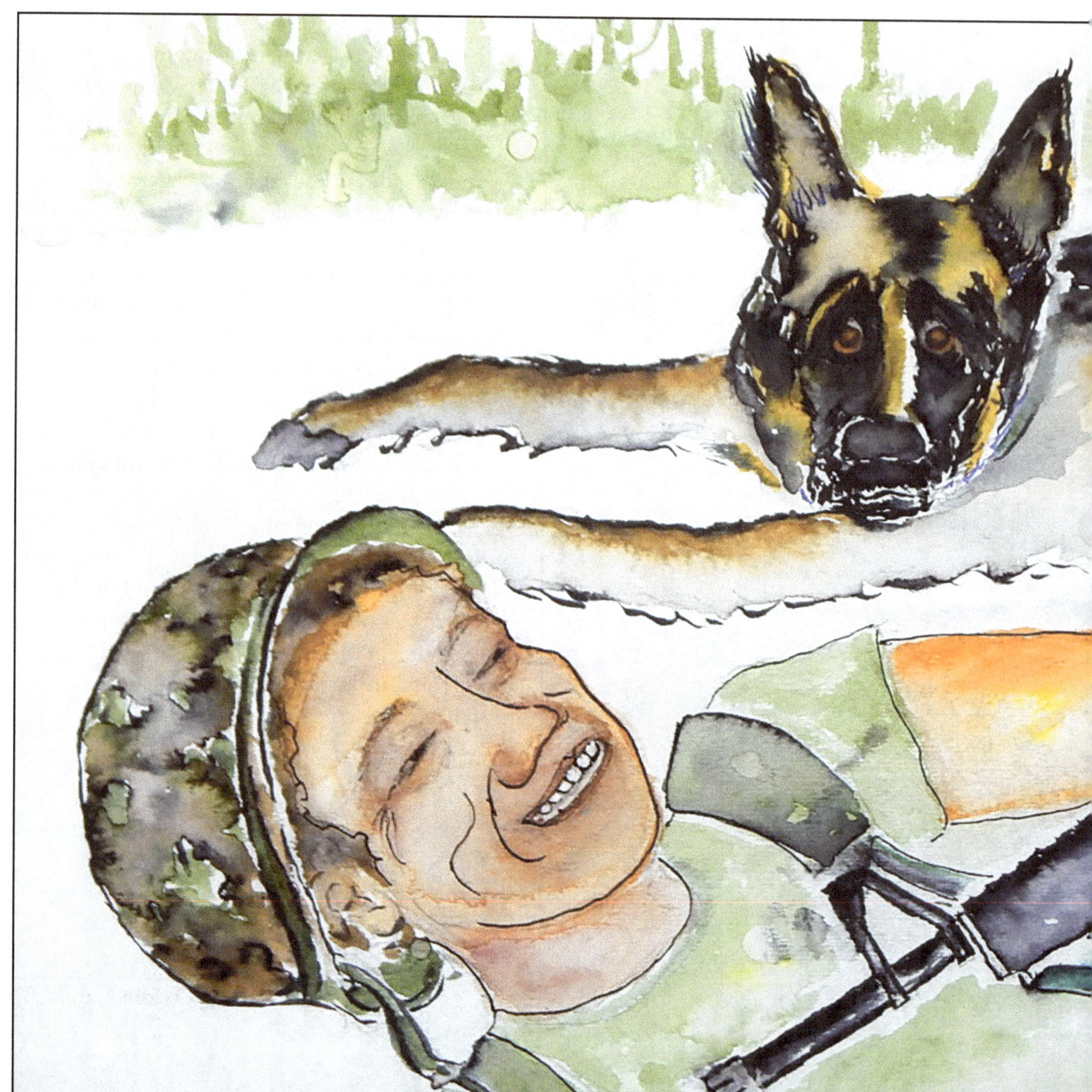

The next day, we exchanged a few shots with the enemy, and the trainer was shaken up. He told me that he's never seen this much action. That evening, another sergeant and I set an automatic daisy chain ambush on a trail leading to our night position. An automatic daisy chain consists of a tripwire, a radio battery, detonating cord, and two or more claymore mines. At daybreak, the next morning, we heard the claymores go off. I and about five others, along with the dog and handler bringing up the rear, approached the kill zone and found two bodies with weapons. I noticed excessive blood led back up the trail towards a draw. I knew there was someone else who had to be severely wounded. I signaled the handler to get his dog up in front of me as we were going up the trail.

With the dog in front on a leash long enough to put the handler behind me, we started moving. Suddenly a shot rang out in front. I didn't hear the whiz of the bullet, but I hit the ground. I looked over to my right and stared right into the German Shepherd's eyes, and the fear and uncertainty in his eyes told it all.

"What is going on and what am I doing here?" the dog seemed to be pleading. One of God's creatures was in a situation not of his making.

I looked at the handler and noticed he was scared shitless. I turned on my back and laughed out loud. I found humor in how the poor dog had to put up with all of the fear and uncertainty that the handler was transferring to him. My guys wanted to know what the hell I thought was so funny. I answered that I would tell them later. We continued to look for the wounded enemy and found him dead.

On the way back, I told the guys why I was laughing. They thought it was funny. I also shared it with the captain who also thought it was funny.

We put the dog team on the next chopper out. I meant no disrespect on other dog teams. I know they saved many lives and were invaluable in finding and exploring enemy tunnels.

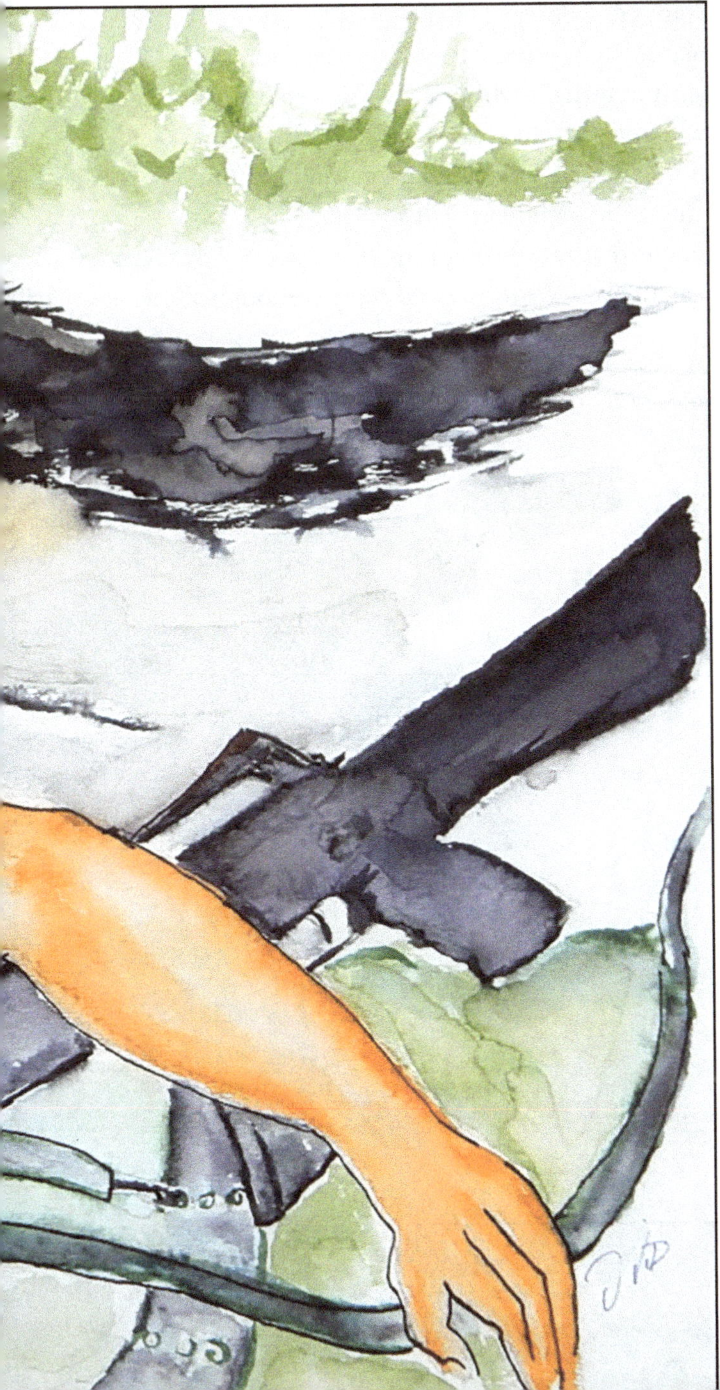

Always loved dogs, and always will.

Ovidio Garcia 39

The Puking Incident

I don't remember the date or the CO involved, but it was in 1971 with the 173rd. It was just before noon and the company had set up to await a hot meal.

Just before the choppers came in with our meal and mail, I was listening to Paul Harvey on the Armed Forces Radio Network, and he had started his program with "and now about our debacle in Vietnam."

I thought to myself "Well that's great! I might die in a debacle, ain't that some shit!"

The choppers brought in the hot meal, a slab of canned ham between two slices of white bread and a small carton of warm milk. The CO said that he didn't like canned ham or warm milk. I ate the ham sandwich.

After the choppers left, we started saddling up. The CO came over with the map to tell me where we were going. As he was talking to me, I was putting on my gear, and with no warning at all I spewed out a strong, steady geyser of puke right into the Captain's chest. I was as surprised as he was.

We stared goggle-eyed at each other, and I did it again. Right after, I felt nauseous, and my bowels just emptied involuntarily. I lowered my self down, and I could see that most of the men were on the ground writhing and groaning. Only a handful of the men were still standing. The first thought that ran through my mind was a biological attack. "We're screwed now," I thought.

The captain and his radio operator had abstained from eating. The captain called the Tactical Operation Center, and the Battalion surgeon diagnosed it as food poisoning. Medics were flown out and arrived in less than an hour and administered shots to everyone affected.

Of course, during the time in between, the sick, including myself, just lay on the ground retching our stomachs trying to expel food we didn't have anymore.

A few hours later we were back on the trail. That was a meal I'll never forget.

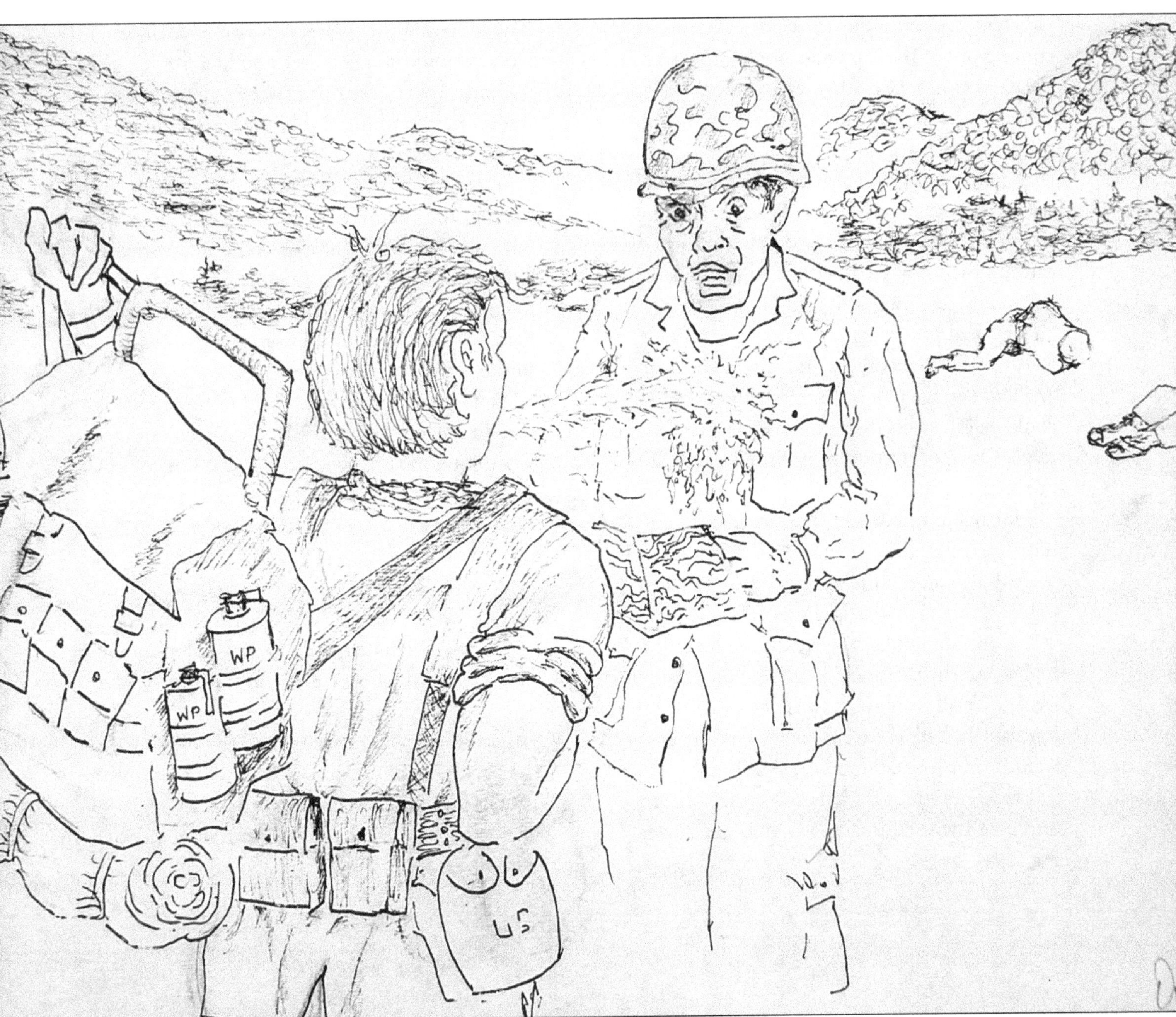

THE BURNING LOG

While on an operation in the highlands of Kon Tum Province, I encountered a situation that caused me consternation for many years. As we were moving single file through the jungle, I was at the rear of the Company column. The Company Commander who was in front of the column called me to come forward. As I moved past one trooper to the other, I spotted smoke coming out of the top of a trooper's rucksack. As I walked closer, I saw that it was a new medic and somehow he had wedged a smoldering log into his pack.

We were under a heavy drizzle, and I could see the burnt end of the log. It was projecting out of the trooper's pack, and the raindrops were causing the smoke. I asked the soldier where he got it, and he said that it came from an H&I area we had passed earlier that day. H&I was an acronym for Harassment and Interdiction, an artillery barrage that a Company Commander could call in at his discretion on suspected enemy targets, real or not. It was also used to confirm our location.

I looked at him, then the log and back at him again and asked why he was carrying it. He replied: "To start a fire when we stop for the night." He was shivering. I was cold to the bone. The Central Highlands were unusually cold at night, and the continuous drizzle only made it worse. We all wore wool sweaters under our shirts but usually took them off during the day as we went from being cold to hot.

I thought about the miserable night before and how I wished I had been any other place but here.

I checked his equipment, which was in no danger of being damaged. The smoke was not a giveaway of our position. We were an infantry unit trudging through the jungle where noise discipline was an impossibility with all our moving and stopping. At any other time, I would have told him to get rid of it right there. Knowing that the weather and absence of dry wood would not allow us to build a fire, his need and my hope for warmth later at night overrode my military training. I told the trooper to carry on and walked away smiling to myself.

At this particular time in the war, it seemed to me that the enemy was avoiding contact, as were our commanders. And who could blame them? They wanted to avoid casualties, ours. The lull in enemy contact could have been because of the Paris peace talks or the rumor of the unit's return to the USA at the end of the year.

Many times since then I told myself this was merely reflective of the war. We started Gung Ho and ended up trying to survive. I once came across a handwritten sign at a Special Forces camp that read:

> We came because we believed.
> We left because we were disillusioned.
> We return because we are lost.
> We die because we are committed.

I know that sign spoke for all the NCO Corp, the backbone of the U.S. Army. We could see the damage this protracted war without a victory was having on our Army and we knew it would take a long time to repair it.

A glimpse of the overall sit (situation).

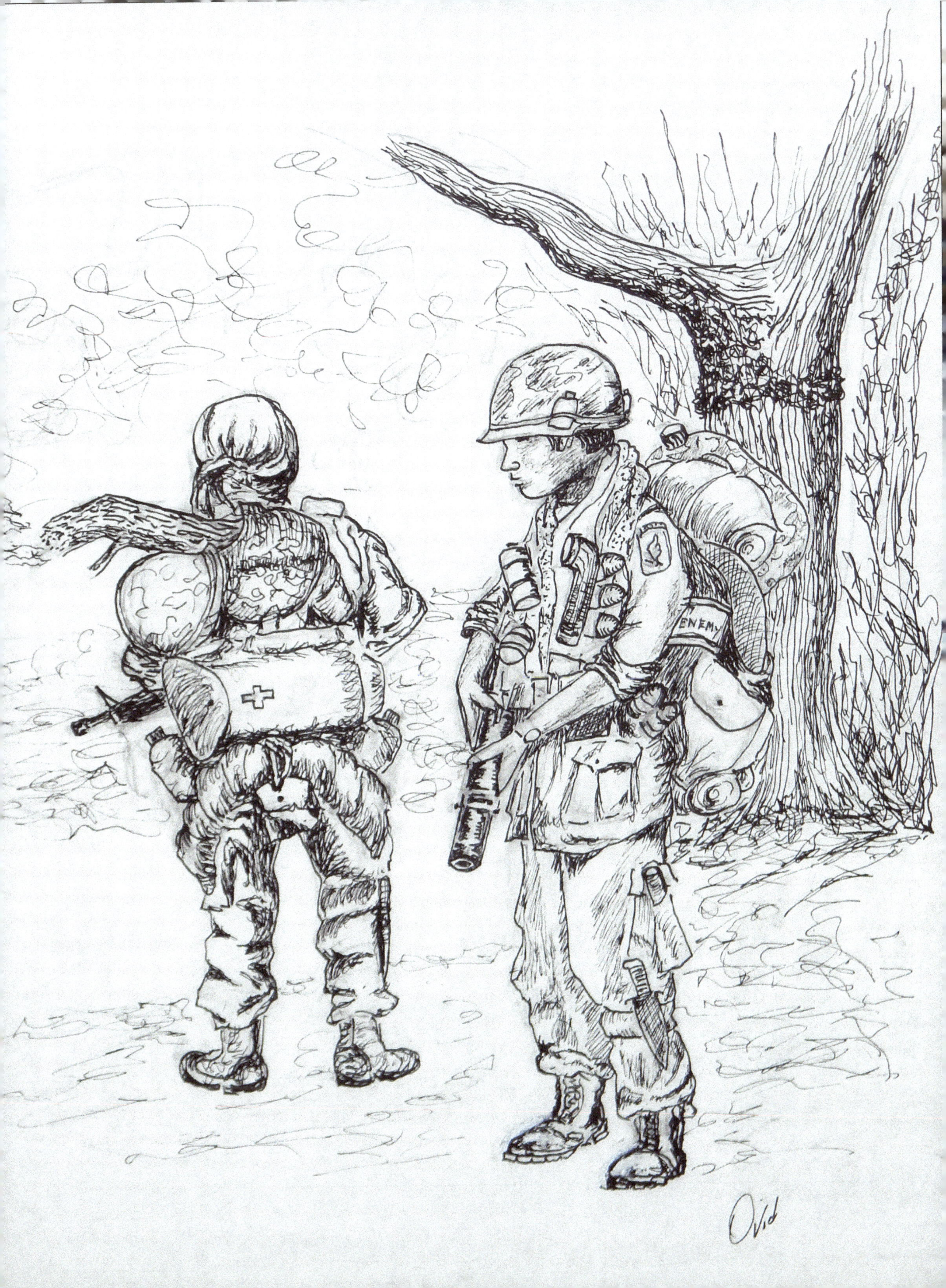

ENEMY